SIX DEGREES OF IMPACT:

Breaking Corporate Glass

A CUTTER ENTERPRISES BOOK

Cover design: EPCO Communications
Editors: Cheryl Nagle & Tara Phillips
Illustrators: Lissette Bayala & Jan ter Haar
Cover Photographer: Phil Stein

ISBN #0-9660315-4-7

SIX DEGREES OF IMPACT:

Breaking Corporate Glass

Anthony C. Gruppo
Monique ter Haar

WARNING! A slingshot is not a toy. *Six Degrees of Impact* is strongly recommended to achieve accurate aim and hit target objectives. Misuse or carelessness may cause serious injury and result in permanent damage to vision.

This book is dedicated to all the people who had an impact on our lives...our mentors and heroes. You taught us to see the world as futurists; to honor the past, respect the present, and create the future. You are our inspiration to make every day a new day. You insist we live untied, undefeated, and unscored upon.

Grab Your Slingshot and Come with Us!

Breaking new ground in business today requires breaking traditional corporate glass to create a high impact zone. Success is no longer achieved simply by thinking out of the box, integrating systems, and planning strategically. It demands we break traditional corporate glass and install new panes to produce vision and success.

Six Degrees of Impact provides perspectives and strategies that bring you insight into the real issues impacting positive change and growth. Like having a consultant in the palm of your hand, this framework gives you the tools to build and manage your organizational future. The *Six Degrees* framework is built on six high impact zones: leadership, strategic positioning, research and development, marketing, human resources, and outcomes. These perspectives remove glass ceilings and provide you with a glass floor that insures both personal and professional growth. With a solid and powerful glass floor in place, you will create the long-term vision and real-life strategies necessary to achieve futuristic goals.

Six Degrees of Impact will show you how to break corporate glass and build organizational success. Step up and begin breaking your corporate glass to build personal and organizational achievement. Challenge yourself, change your perspective, and increase your vision. Apply the *Six Degrees* to your world and you will evolve to a level others will seek to duplicate. You will gain the fuel critical to become a quality, profitable vehicle on the fast track to success.

Impact Zones

LEADERSHIP

STRATEGIC POSITIONING

FORWARD

...and above all.

LEADERSHIP

The 1st Degree

<u>LEADERSHIP</u>

The 1st Degree

Leadership is the most critical zone of the *Six Degrees* and the one all others are built upon. It distinguishes those who manage to simply sustain business from those who overachieve in every environment they enter. The overachievers of life embody an entrepreneurial spirit challenging traditional boundaries and breaking corporate glass.

In the great debate about the difference between leaders and managers, we have always found leaders speak to opportunity and managers speak to activity. As technology begins to provide more efficient delivery of tasks, managers will be led into extinction. The following leadership perspectives supply you with a focus on creating ownership cultures and growth opportunities for people wherever they stand.

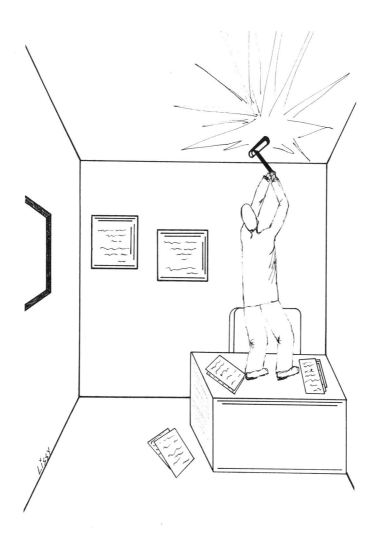

THE GLASS FLOOR

THE GLASS FLOOR

Prepare to break some glass. Most will agree that traditional business models have been built on a hierarchy of systems and titles. These vertical structures place responsibility at the top and cast long shadows of confusion on the subjects below. To achieve the speed and competitive edge necessary to respond to changes in any business market, we must replace glass ceilings with glass floors providing a total perspective on our surroundings.

Although they may vary in degree and subtlety, glass ceilings are still common in today's workplace. Glass ceilings were traditionally gender-focused, but they can also limit ownership based on ethnicity, age, or any asset detracting power from leadership. Glass ceilings encourage corporate racism, which exists when ideas are discounted because of an individual's title, background, or lack of traditional qualifications as an "expert". Environments with glass ceilings may encourage people to express their ideas, but the ideas of the creators are replaced with the face of a "bigger" title. Strategies like outright plagiarism and repackaging concepts limit ownership to the top, causing the opportunity for individual and organizational growth to become lost.

When we base our survival instincts and decisions on titles, ignorance threatens our survival. Replace certainty with curiosity and eliminate corporate racism.

Contrary to popular belief, leaders are not always aware of how their actions perpetuate corporate racism. During a meeting where a leader had invited his colleagues to speak on their areas of expertise to a client, we saw the glass ceiling in action. The leader had placed himself first on the meeting agenda. Upon closing the discussion of his issues, the leader called it a day before handing the meeting over to his colleagues. Essentially, the leader had closed the doors for business before allowing his colleagues to step onto the floor. The energy in the room dropped and the leader's colleagues were left de-motivated. The lack of continuity caused the client to feel as if they had been left with the second string team for the rest of the game.

This scenario can occur for a variety of reasons. The leader may not have confidence in their colleague's ability to address issues or add value to the discussion. In some cases, we have seen the ceiling dropped on people's heads because the leader fears others will dilute their authority or have greater impact on a situation. In any case, the result was the same. The credibility of those who followed the leader had been undermined.

The glass floor serves as a powerful magnifying lens to removing corporate racism and examining a path of true performance. Use the *Six Degrees of Impact* to break your vertical corporate glass and stand on a horizontal platform giving you a 360-degree perspective on opportunity. If you build your business on the strength of everyone's ability and performance, you will build a glass floor that continues to deliver consistent performance and vision. When you stand on a glass floor, you will travel through life with the ability to see the future as clearly as you see the past. Regardless of the failures, you will always be able to see the opportunities of the future. Always accept change for the perspective and wisdom it brings and never call it a day!

ROCK BOTTOM

ROCK BOTTOM

In business, we see various levels of the bottom. Early in our careers, we heard about hitting rock bottom. We also heard the stories of those who had the misfortune of falling from success to disaster. There are certainly different degrees of bottom. Some people hit bottom much sooner than others. The middle ground for one may be the bottom for another. Rock bottom should be considered a beginning and not an end.

There are those so beaten they have to look up to see bottom. They constantly concentrate on disappointments instead of opportunities. Our *Six Degrees* is the ladder to climb from the bottom to the top. Think of the *Six Degrees* as the rungs on your ladder. They can be effective both on a personal and professional level. We often hear about the career ladder and the ladder to success. They are terms meaning little without a system to sustain us through the eventual bouts with the bottom.

Consider the tale of two professionals. Over a career spanning twenty-two years, these producers consistently finished at the top of the leader board. Their client retention level had never fallen below ninety-five percent. Then, in one year, they lost two major accounts. The market was extremely competitive and product lines had become stagnant. They had accepted new challenges, adding to an already taxing schedule. Four out of five of their projects had ended in defeat. These two were definite candidates for the rock bottom blues.

Simultaneously, they implemented the *Six Degrees* and the result was incredible. They assumed greater personal and corporate leadership and communicated openly with each other about their losses. They shared with the entire organization their plans for recovery and success. They marketed their skills and those of their colleagues. Strategic planning became their personal pathway. Jointly, they assembled a team of tough colleagues to venture into new areas of research and development. They capitalized on their shared human resources to climb through the unknown. As a team, they determined what outcomes they needed and never looked back. They built their ladder to success using the *Six Degrees* as the rungs.

Instead of hitting rock bottom, they rocked production. The producers finished on top and the team had prospects galore for the next season. The organization found new opportunities in research and development work. The strategic plan built long-range vision and human resources was at improved efficiency.

So, what is rock bottom? It appears to be different for everyone. Rock bottom is the place where it appears all options have been eliminated. There are always options if we move to meet the challenge. Challenge is the essence of growth and the feet of the ladder. Challenge stabilizes the climb to new achievement. Everyone slips, but the great ones never look down.

Rock bottom is not the end of anything. It is the beginning of everything. New energy and knowledge come from the bottom, where every mistake becomes tomorrow's opportunity.

Never allow others to bring you to their level of rock bottom. Never fear the risk of new enterprise. Believe in the challenge and seek the rewards of energetic achievement. You are the rock and the bottom is the first rung on your ladder to success.

THE ESCAPE ARTISTS

THE ESCAPE ARTISTS

We both realized we wanted to be escape artists when we were kids. Since Houdini was our idol, we often searched for opportunities to trap ourselves in seemingly death-defying situations. We would climb a tree and leap to a neighboring treetop without ever touching the ground. We would ask others to tie ropes around our wrists and attempt to free ourselves. Picking locks was our recreational sport. All we needed was another dangerous death trap from which to escape.

We believe entrepreneurs are the escape artists of the modern-day business world. They have escaped failure through their entrepreneurial insight. Their vision sees past the locks, ropes, and chains of preconceived limitations. In their mind's eye, they can look at a changing business climate and see an unmet need as an opportunity for the great escape.

Escape artists test themselves by going where others wouldn't dare for fear of becoming trapped. Performing the stunt is not about defying death, seeking glory, or counting the money. It is about building a better trap and planning the ultimate escape. Every day, they trade money and glory for insight and respect. After each great escape, they search for a tougher trap from which to free themselves.

To be successful in life and business, we must continue to trap ourselves with new challenges in search of the great escape.

Step into the mindset of an escape artist and continually place yourself into tighter and tighter traps. Although others will look at the trap and see only the risk, you will see the opportunity for escape glaring right back at you. Escape your preconceptions and you will create your own reality. Do not fear any emotional straight jacket challenging your inspiration and never rely on luck.

Each time you set another trap, you will become smarter. Every time you escape, you create understanding and opportunity for others. Others will seek your counsel as they plan their escapes. Eventually, the master escape trick is to disappear into thin air while others bow to a standing ovation.

Although many believe escape artists are driven by the dare of the trap, they are really attracted to the freedom of the escape. The greatest threat to an escape artist is their self-confidence turning into arrogance. The best escape artists never believed they would make it in "Hollywood", the land of success and achievement. Never fear losing fortune or fame. Instead, focus on the vision to see alternatives and bring the courage to attempt the impossible. Even after the stunt is over, the thrill remains because the search for the great escape is never-ending.

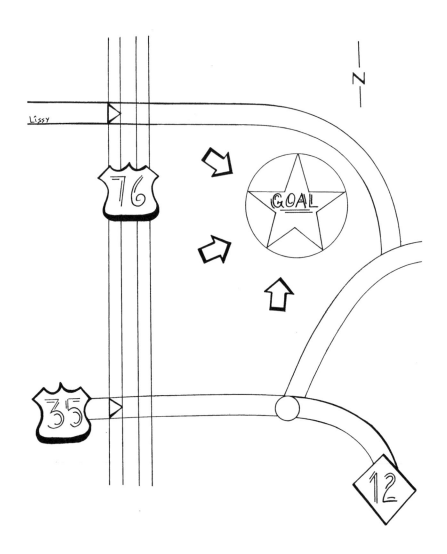

ACCESSORIES NOT INCLUDED

ACCESSORIES NOT INCLUDED

Everyone has a professional skill package. When we first received our skill packages, there were no accessories included. The lessons we learned from our mentors formulated our skill package. Although we have accumulated accessories over time, we can't rely on them to charge our batteries and keep us moving. Many professionals pack models and systems, spending a lifetime collecting accessories. The overachiever evolves by expanding their skill package through constant mentoring.

Every day, mentors are influenced by their desire to acquire new skills and achieve peak performance. The best mentors we know never stop mentoring themselves.

Mentors face challenge knowing their accessories are not included. They assume they know nothing and they go from there. As mentors, we must equip others with survival skills that will not leave them dependent on their accessories.

Mentors are master guides at searching for insight and remembering the lessons learned from past teachers. They are able to see into individual needs and move quickly to meet them. They understand there is more than one path to reach a goal and are always advocates of action. However, mentors realize there are times when action accomplishes nothing and nothing might be the best thing to do. It is action taken, while others pause to gather their accessories, which advances ideas into realities.

Ideals are achieved when individuals are charged with the courage to extend their viewpoints and leave behind any unnecessary baggage. Whether building a new business or shifting leadership roles, uncertainty about the future creates a desire to grab onto something concrete…systems, models, plans, and charts. Transitions cause us to focus on directed activities that establish specific boundaries and bridges. Transitions can become hazardous intersections of change, which cause us to lose sight of the vision.

Periods of transition are frequently a time when we should remember to travel light. Insecurities about their own abilities to cross the intersection can lead mentors to respond more like crossing guards than wilderness guides. The end result can be the difference between creating obedient children or corporate renegades.

There are some simple guidelines every coach can follow to increase their impact as a mentor. An impact mentor blends creativity with reason. They add emotion and energy to the logic needed to find answers. The mentor searches for the answer with the apprentice without ever taking too much pride in what has been learned. Creative greed only results in failure to achieve the goal. As mentors, we assume the risk of responsibility and pass on the reward. Impact is our reward.

As long as we continue to think through the obstacles with a sense of urgency, we will achieve every goal with an impact advantage.

Strength comes in knowing what you want to create and learning about new worlds.

Failure to see what can be learned overlooks the humility in learning. It is humility in teaching that realizes growth.

Movement driven by creative energy adds to the mentoring magic. As long as the momentum continues, the mentor will never have to struggle over when they should let go. If there is humility in the mutual momentum achieved, there is no limit to the growth. Growth can be stifled if we begin to rely on accessories to deliver results instead of our skill package. Consider the professional who believes models and charts contain all the answers. Their structure will limit adaptability, and ultimately, growth. Mentoring models are no exception.

If we continually push others to expand their skill packages, we will improve our own ability to accomplish previously unachievable goals. A piece of our future is in the hands of those we guide.

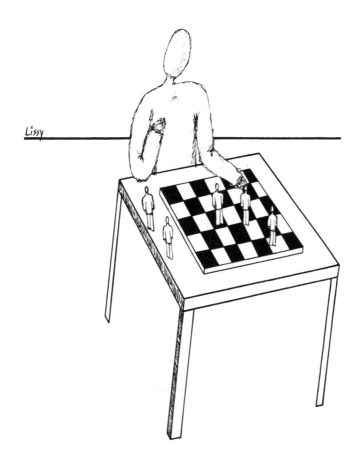

THE TOR-MENTOR

THE TOR-MENTOR

We have met great mentors and, unfortunately, our fair share of "Tor-mentors". A corporate Tor-mentor has a tremendous negative impact on outcomes. They constantly move people, both emotionally and physically, like pieces on a game board. The Tor-mentor does not realize how they crush positive outcomes with their behavior.

In one instance, we were invited guests of a CEO for the unveiling of their new organizational structure. As we sat in the meeting, we watched the torture of colleagues occur right before our eyes. As the CEO introduced a member of management, each was met with a backhanded compliment. Instead of praising her colleagues, she would reference a flaw.

The Tor-mentor toys with their subject's emotions in a torture cell that shatters confidence and trust.

Sadly, this was only the beginning of the torture. One phase of the consulting project involved personality profile testing. Each leader of the organization was profiled for the positions being considered. When used properly, this can be a powerful tool for assisting colleagues in identifying their individual strengths. In the hands of the Tor-mentor, it became a means of continuing the agony of her colleagues.

There was one colleague vying to be selected for a key leadership position. She had worked hard to acquire the skills needed to move to the next level. Her test results clearly showed she was the person for the promotion. We met with the Tor-mentor and agreed to set up a meeting with her colleague to announce the selection.

On the day of the meeting, we waited with the Tor-mentor for her colleague to arrive. When the door opened, the Tor-mentor appeared to be pensive and serious concern could be seen on her face. The colleague picked up on these cues and thought there was something terribly wrong. Her facial expressions and body language were typical of someone who thought they were in trouble. When the Tor-mentor spoke, she explained the test was in and she was sad to announce the colleague had received the position. Then, the Tor-mentor laughed and relished at the fact that she had placed her colleague in the torture cell.

Tor-mentors love to play with the feelings of their colleagues. They receive pleasure from humiliating and teasing their co-workers. They use power to flex their ego and make up for their own insecurity. Immediately, we came to the defense of the tortured colleague and reaffirmed our confidence in her selection. Unfortunately, it was too late because she had already been cheated of her celebration.

There are steps we can take to escape from the dungeon of corporate Tor-mentors. First, never tolerate their behavior. Immediately, express your disappointment and frustration with their actions. Second, help them understand the demoralizing effect of their behavior. Third, remember you are the owner of your opportunities. If you think like an owner, the Tor-mentor can never beat down your spirit.

THE TIGHTROPE

THE TIGHTROPE

When we were children, we loved to ice skate. We would gather with our friends after school and skate on the local pond, which was located in the one street town of Bangor Junction. This natural rink was also the playground of the Finelli brothers.

Pat and Lou Finelli were legends in our area. They were both tremendous athletes. They were the subjects of several town stories. When we first met the Finellis, they were in their early seventies. Neighbors told the story of how Pat would wrestle the carnival strongman whenever the show rolled into town. On one occasion, Pat had actually wrestled a bear at the annual carnival and won. He had even pulled a train car with his teeth. We have clear memories of Pat riding a unicycle around the local park and teaching youngsters weightlifting in his garage.

One Saturday afternoon, we were skating at the pond when we saw something unbelievable. Pat and Lou were suspended in, what appeared to be, thin air. As youngsters, we stood wide-eyed in awe and disbelief. We walked toward this spectacle and found the Finellis actually tightrope walking. They had installed cables from one tree to another. As we approached, they held onto their homemade balance pole and smiled.

For weeks, they taught us the techniques of wire walking. There were four basic rules. First of all, you must place one foot directly in front of the other. Second, you must focus your eyes straight ahead. Third, the wire will give but never break. Finally, never and they stressed never, look down. We never completely mastered the tightrope, but we have benefited from their lessons throughout our lives.

Achievement and the ability to meet challenge are like tightrope walking. Place one goal in front of the other as you take steps toward your vision. When you stay on course, you will discover balance no matter how thin your opportunities may appear.

We need to stay focused on our mission and vision. One second guess can produce doubt and create failure. Failure will surely occur, but energy and perseverance prevents the cable from breaking. When we let go of our comfort area and walk the tightrope over the uncertainty of challenge, we must never look back. If we look back or down, we will be forced to fall from our advantage point.

A colleague in support of our strategic plan is the best balance pole for our tightrope walk to success. Pat and Lou cheered for each other. As junior circus performers, we all wanted to make it from one tree to the other. If we fell, everyone hurried to see if we were injured. Modern day leadership crews could certainly use a few tightrope lessons from the Finelli brothers. Life is a tightrope where we can balance challenge if we focus and realize success is only one step away.

CORPORATE COURT

CORPORATE COURT

Anyone who has witnessed a case tried in corporate court knows it has very little to do with justice. Corporate court can be held anywhere. It needs no courtroom or office. Most corporate courts conduct public trials and don't require the defendants to be present. As a matter of fact, they are usually not invited. The jury knows the charges before the defendant.

Evidence entered can be secondary to the final verdict. Public opinion will decide the verdict unless the judge disallows unsubstantiated evidence.

If corporate judges allow rumor and conjecture, the workplace will become known as a place for mock trials. These leaders will lose respect and their rulings will result in zero to negative impact. Ineffective leaders are like hanging judges to the innocent colleague. They neglect their responsibility to give every defendant a fair corporate trial.

Corporate divorce cases can particularly become a drain on energy and are often rooted in jealousy. They frequently involve a client or colleague who is exploring alternatives and developing new relationships. If confidence levels are low, they can strain the relationship. It doesn't matter whether the lack of confidence is in oneself or in someone else. Eventually, it all comes back to our ability to deal with adversity. Find the courage to stand face to face with conflict and directly address all parties involved and you will be able to settle issues without a lengthy drawn-out trial.

Watch how some businesses respond to a client or colleague who is shopping for other candi"dates" to meet their needs. They act as if they had just been betrayed. They don't realize the pressure they are putting on themselves to provide a remedy for every circumstance. The strain of trying to be everything to a client or colleague is unrealistic and suffocates ambition. Possessiveness only fosters limited vision and isolates learning. Eventually, the organization will fail because it ends up spreading itself too thin.

Even though you don't have all of the answers in your head, you can still provide them. Build partnerships and alliances to broker positive solutions for your clients and colleagues. We have an obligation to ourselves and to others to encourage the exploration of new ideas and opportunities. The following four objectives should be focused on when listening to a case and mentoring other corporate counsel:

♦ Realize mistakes are opportunities to teach.
♦ Remove judgement and seek to understand the person.
♦ Help others to see and achieve their dreams.
♦ Never attend public trials without the defendant present.

Spend less time looking for crimes to pass judgement on and more time on finding solutions. When attacks are made against partners or alliances, we must defend our allegiances and deliver on commitment by looking for diversity rather than differences. There is a wealth of learning all around us we fail to tap into if we assume only one of us can have all the answers. Answers are not always found under the "proper" labels. Always assume the person you are talking to knows more than either of you realizes.

When the conversation concentrates on new business and life opportunities rather than the latest rumor, there is an immediate shift to a more positive environment. Listening becomes focused on support instead of slander. Interaction will create solutions, not sacrificial offerings to the rumor gods.

Choose to grow young, not to grow old. See the opportunity over the ordeal and you will enjoy a panoramic view of business and life.

Consume yourself with positive energy and creative madness. Listen closely and you will build the future on the energy and ideas of your clients and colleagues. The desire to overcome the impossible is an invitation to search for opportunity.

BACKSTAGE AT THE LIFE

BACKSTAGE AT THE LIFE

If you have ever watched a performer prepare for a show, you know many drive themselves to the point of insanity before they step onto the stage. It doesn't matter if they are performing under a circus tent or at a convention center. They put pressure on themselves by thinking of the time and money the audience has invested to be entertained. Every detail becomes a factor in delivering a memorable and positive experience for the audience.

Consider the stage of life. It is the best stage show we know. Backstage is the place where the preparation for the show begins and the actors get psyched. It is where we run through our lines, put on our costumes, and overcome our fears.

When you get ready to walk onto the stage of life, prepare to walk out on stage with your best performance and beware of the props.

We've often seen performers walk out on stage with an armload of props. Their plan is to entertain with slide shows, cartoons, handouts, flipcharts, promotional kits, and a battery of questions for the audience. Without realizing it, the performer has forfeited their chance for rave reviews by focusing their act on the props. Substitute the props with passion and you will deliver your message with impact every time.

We know one performer who was an award winner. She had been an overachiever all of her life. While preparing to go on stage, she met one of her toughest challenges. She couldn't remember her lines and had lost all confidence in herself. Her ability to deliver her performance with passion disappeared and she wouldn't even come out of her dressing room. She had lost her ability to dream. She began to search for someone who could give her the key to overcome her fears and unlock her dreams.

Then one day she opened the door and, for a brief moment, stepped out onto the stage of life again. When people saw her, she began to realize she had been missed. The enthusiasm she felt when she spoke from the heart with courage, compassion, and commitment excited both her and everyone around her. She finally realized we all write our own scripts in life and she began to write hers. The person holding the key had been in the mirror all along.

Think of every day as a premiere event and the world as your audience. Prepare to walk out on stage with nothing in hand and deliver your script. Engage every day as your own stage production and strive to deliver your best performance. The best shows don't use cue cards and dialogue boxes. They take people on a journey filled with opportunity. In turn, the opportunity provides new challenges, strengthening your ability to deliver an award-winning performance. Every show is the performance of your lifetime. Always give them your best act…no act at all.

STRATEGIC POSITIONING

The 2nd Degree

STRATEGIC POSITIONING

The 2nd Degree

In the *Second Degree,* we share our perspectives on positioning your business to deliver on your goals and dreams. Strategic Positioning guides the direction of your future and transforms your dreams into designs for success.

The first step in knowing where you are going is looking at where you have been. Evaluate the achievements you have gained in each of the *Six Degrees* and the risks of your current endeavors. Consider everything you do well and where you can improve in each of the degrees. Before developing a strategic plan, conduct the same analysis on your competitors. Once you have developed a strategic plan utilizing the *Six Degrees* model, you are ready to move the plan into action through methods establishing clear communication, project management, and performance accountability.

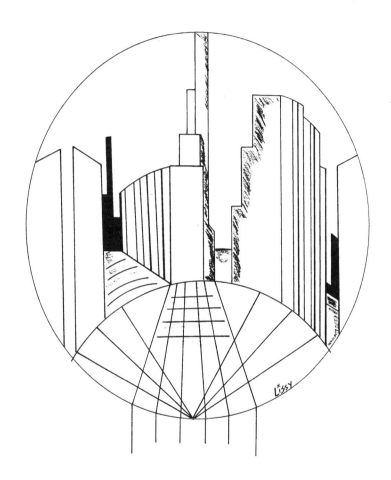

WELCOME TO CIRCULAR CITY

WELCOME TO CIRCULAR CITY

Most business professionals have heard the cries for top management support as a necessary element for driving change. Without support from the top, any efforts to change won't have the necessary value and priority to make the shift.

Let us take you to a place where change leaves people standing where they started because they are led in circles. Movement only occurs to reduce the guilt of stagnation. People choose destinations with confident relief because they have already arrived. Committees meet for six months to write a mission statement and marketing efforts are solely focused on selling more of the same product to the same clients. Welcome to Circular City!

When we first entered the village of Circular City, we learned outsiders were not welcome and new ideas were discouraged. Lack of top management support and direction had led the village into isolation. Isolation had reversed the goals of organizational success and removed them from the marketplace. Instead of venturing out into the world for new opportunities, the villagers preyed on each other. Their primary motive was ego, and crimes of cowardice prevailed. Agendas had shifted from organizational to individual and change was driven by struggles for power.

Sections of the village had tried to improve by totally restructuring and replacing their warriors. This strategy resulted in internal attacks and decisions became focused on persecuting other villagers.

Rightsizing was a downgrading experience, which had infected the entire village with alienation. They soon realized that progress would result from focus and direction rather than speed of change.

Knowing this, they chose to build the village back up instead of tearing it down. The elders knew it would take a strong leader to recognize the abilities of the villagers and build on their strengths and opportunities.

Recognizing the need for focused change, the board of directors, like a tribunal of elders, went in search of a new chief. They knew speed and decisiveness was critical because the village was incredibly vulnerable when the chief was missing in action. Simply placing warm bodies or absent minds on the throne would not guarantee success. They called in a wizard to help them search for a leader with intelligence, courage, and heart.

When the new chief arrived, people immediately began to wonder where he came from and what he might do. Rumor had it he was a bricklayer and many questioned what he knew about leading a village. He heard the rumor and decided to share some of the skills he had learned as a bricklayer. He explained that when building a solid pathway, it is important to plot the lines, level the surface, and fill in the gaps. When replacing an old path with a new one, old bricks that are still strong can be used again. He led them to believe as long as they start where they are, use what they have, and do what they can, together they would build a strong path to their future.

Today, Circular City is a place where the road to achievement is laid with the bricks of focus and direction. Progress is created out of the willingness to reinvent and the desire to evolve to the next level.

THE BLIND VISIONARY

THE BLIND VISIONARY

There is a place where dreams are inspired and vision is created. Anyone is invited to go there. The only requirement is being able to see with an open mind. The flight of discovery is not in seeking new landscapes, but in seeing through new eyes. If you can see and speak your vision through intuitive thinking, others will know the future as you have seen it. It is true, seeing is believing.

Along the path to your vision, you may encounter blind visionaries. Visioning is almost counterintuitive to the blind visionary. Believing they have seen it all, they are usually able to tell you why a concept failed in the past. Their vision is in their hindsight, which appears very clearly once the vision has been achieved.

Although they may believe their own sight to be 20/20, the vision of the blind visionary becomes blurred because they are unable to see past the idea to the potential. Without intention, the blind visionary has the ability to fill a room with so much smoke that you can't even see the mirrors. The opportunity becomes lost in the activity. There are ways to utilize the talents of a blind visionary to everyone's advantage. Allow them to serve as a devil's advocate. Their ability to ask the difficult questions is an asset during tactical planning sessions and can prevent hardship at the end of the task. Over time, they may see that visions achieved were once only ideas conceived.

Blind visionaries will seek to outfit a mission with systems, models, and plans they feel are necessary to succeed before they confirm whether a project fits their vision. They will accessorize the project with new pencil sets and project planners for everyone before evaluating the opportunity with a business plan. If we allow the systems to power the vision, our focus will become limited to the short-term objectives. Utilize a business plan initially to respond to the vision by addressing financial resources, implementation strategies, marketing models, and staff training needs.

Accessories are not required to move forward. If we delay our response, we will be too slow and indistinguishable in the marketplace. Use the speed of your vision to generate momentum and the models will follow to support you.

As you venture out in search of vision, there will only be a few who follow and isolation may set in. In the mind of the leader, isolation is the solitary sound you hear while standing on the edge of discovery. Your vision will provide others with the clarity to see through the fray of everyday tasks.

Never focus your personal or business plans on getting to a certain position or status. You will only cheat yourself as plans designed for getting "there" only blind vision with task and mangle creativity. Task is a one-person vehicle, leaving the traveler with no one but himself or herself to talk to. Vision is a vehicle with room for everyone involved.

Step into your vision and travel to a destination where dreams become reality and achievements are mile markers on the road to the future. As a tour guide of life, the visionary understands the destination of any vision is the journey itself.

THE CHESS BOARD

THE CHESS BOARD

Think of the members of your board of directors as the pieces you position in a game of chess. Each is equipped with various skills, knowledge, and abilities, providing you with a set of unique resources, which strengthen your ability to move in many directions at all levels of the game. It doesn't matter whether an individual serves as a warrior or cannon fodder. Players with multiple abilities provide you with a team of fearless heroes whose efforts are coordinated in the campaign for your organization's perseverance.

Typically, a board of directors consists of a mixture of professionals from the worlds of finance, law, technology, and industry. However, they may appear to be nothing more than a collection of career experts showing up for meetings like tourists going to Florida on a holiday.

Your board needs energetic visionaries, deal makers, and futurists. Create a global advisory board to target marketing and development opportunities. Build the board of directors to serve as the force behind strategic positioning. If you retain community leadership, strategic positioning power, research and development, marketing minds, and resource muscle, you will generate diverse outcomes. These dreamers and schemers will create cunning plans and strategies in a world dominated by chess masters.

Leaders checkmate themselves before their competition does.

The rules of conduct for a board of directors are no different than the game rules for the pieces on a chessboard. Give, Get, or Get Off! These commandments place the same expectations for accountability and production on board members as they do on anyone else in the organization. If a board member doesn't hunt and gather new resources for the organization, they should be airlifted out to make room for fresh troops.

The recruitment and screening of board members is really no different from hiring talent for other positions in an organization. Be clear and direct with candidates about your expectations for their commitment and performance. Provide prospective candidates with opportunities to learn about the organization prior to placing them on the board. This allows you to assess their speed, responsiveness, and interests. In addition, you are preparing them to hit the ground running when they start.

Managing the board's focus requires clear direction on the following core leadership functions:

- Community Relations
- Revenue Development
- Advisors to the Leadership Crew
- Organizational Focus
- Strategic Positioning
- Cooperative Partnerships
- Mentors and Coaches
- Perpetuation and Succession
- Board Accountability

♦ Research and Development

Develop defined goals and strategies for impact in each of these ten areas. If you outline a clear path for future business targets, you will provide the board with an operational framework to move quickly and decisively. Move plans into action with these core decision-making principles:

♦ Demand a sense of urgency
♦ Weigh the risks against the rewards
♦ Isolate key decisions needing immediate resolution
♦ Determine the consequences of decision postponement
♦ Create detailed options for future investment revenue and recruitment

If you utilize these performance guidelines and strategies, your board will move resources effectively to achieve future growth and positive margin.

THE RUNAWAY

THE RUNAWAY

This story begins with a dedicated and well meaning leadership team preparing for the annual corporate strategic planning retreat. Everyone was excited about the event and ideas were flowing freely among the merry band of managers. They arrived at the conference center and began their quest for the ultimate plan. Three days later, they returned to their base of operations and cheerfully communicated their plan to their colleagues. In three months, the plan suffered its first setback. The leaders had discovered one of their band was missing and had become a corporate runaway.

Corporate runaways fear the challenge of their goals. When accountability knocks, they pack up their objectives, become runaways, and hitchhike to the nearest excuse route.

After returning from a strategic planning session, most organizations forget to monitor their plan to make sure it is following their proposed objectives. They allow the routine of the day to stall the reality of the future. Often times, we miss the signals a potential runaway sends prior to skipping out on their goals. These signals may be a constant changing of completion dates without a solid reason or the inability to interact with colleagues working on the same strategic plan. Although the runaway may appear interested in the work of others, they are aloof when dealing with their charge. Runaways have no idea where they are going, but believe it is better to flee than to face the challenges.

If we create detailed action plans providing runaways with success on an ongoing basis, we may keep them focused so they will want to remain at home. Organize strategic follow-up meetings with purpose and facilitate forward movement. Allow everyone involved in the program to give reports and updates of their progress. Be tough if they begin to fall off the project pace. Strategic delivery is problematic if proposed timetables are not followed. Make sure everyone understands each of the strategic planners is an important member of the team.

Daily routine is often more comfortable than the unknown challenge. As the leader, you must do your best to integrate daily operations with future strategy. If everyone cannot see how the strategy will benefit future operations, you probably have a weak plan. Most colleagues become runaways because they were not fully committed to the plan from the beginning.

We propose the concept of a strategic benefit plan to build commitment. A strategic benefit plan provides security as results are achieved. If you have good results, the coverage protection for the strategic planner will increase to match the success. If your planners are usually successful at hitting their targets, lower their deductibles and raise their coverage. Deductibles are risk tolerance. A better than average planner should be allowed to take on more risk. Great leaders should be looked at in the same way you would look at insurance. Insure the health of your organization through the hiring of healthy, driven, and focused colleagues.

Cover the strategic planner with a policy protecting them against the accidental injury of a failed goal. Let them know you understand the risk and will cover them against failure with a policy protecting overachievers. If a planner is secure in their abilities, they will assume greater risk and challenge their future performance.

WING-BACKED OR WINGED-BACK

WING-BACKED OR WINGED-BACK

One beautiful fall day, we arrived at a university for an interview with an intern who was willing to work with us on a variety of projects. We both were very excited to have this opportunity because we were convinced an intern would truly support our development efforts. If we could surround ourselves with bright, energetic, and fast-paced talent, we would able to move faster and reach an even greater level of productivity.

Upon entering the student lounge, we sat on a sofa and came face to face with the trusted and business minded wing-backed chair. As we looked at the chair, it stared back at us as if we were long lost cousins. Speed and urgency had just met the slow and the patient. Since we have a stand-up office, this chair looked like a rock seat in the home of a caveman. We knew we were there in search of a *winged-back* being who was faster than light.

We can all recall the time when being wing-backed meant being slow, tedious, and process driven. Those were the ancient or not-so-ancient days of the wing-backed chair. Can you remember sitting in those chairs at the gathering of the business clan? Oh, we thought we were the chosen, sitting on our thrones of knowledge. As young executives, we loved to sit with the elder leaders listening to the stories and dreaming of our time to fly the wing-backed beauty.

Many living rooms are furnished with these symbols of power. If given the choice of a variety of chairs to sit on in a room, many seek to test-drive the stylish wing-backed. They are tall, comfortable, and offer protection to the neck and head. Fathers and mothers would post up in these pillars of parenting and lecture to their children. Now, we wonder if we have totally sacrificed important dialogue for quick decision.

We should combine the experience of the patient wing-backed chair with the speed and decisiveness of the winged-back professional. When matched together, they will produce a skilled flyer that navigates the skies of achievement.

Surround yourself with both the older veterans and the young test pilots of the future. With the right crew in place, the combination of experience and speed can be yours now. You will not have to wait for the years to accrue before you are able to command your own test plane.

Be a student of past projects and programs. Learn from the pilots who flew without the luxury of the modern instruments you so desperately need for your flight. They too had to fly fast and in bad weather. While the young pilot will be a constant throttle challenger, the older pilot will teach them to steady their hand on the throttle to keep the winged-back beast from stalling mid-goal.

Armed with the *Six Degrees*, you will be launched to achievement from the trusted pad of the wing-backed chair. In flight, your skills and decision making will enable you to soar to your destination. There are clear choices you will make to grow these incredible wings, but you will never have to choose between speed and experience. The combination of both will deliver a future that belongs to the fast and the brave, the young and the old.

A funny thing happens when you wear wings. Suddenly, sitting back becomes uncomfortable.

SCOPE IT OUT

SCOPE IT OUT

Every organization experiences the inclination to explore alternative streams of revenue through diversification. As a proven business strategy, diversification has provided fallback positions for survival in rapidly changing business environments. The lure of a new business adventure can be seductive and draw an organization off its course. Like an explorer checking their compass to plan the expedition, a business must view the prospect of a new venture through the scope of their original mission.

To explore potential avenues for diversification, you should first ask yourself and your colleagues what you want to be when you grow up. No joke!

For any goal to be achieved, it must start as a dream, which has invested in it the passion, spirit, and heart of its creators. If you can see it, you can build it. The momentum of your dreams and visions will create the new markets of the future.

Take a look around you to see how your current competitors are building stability and flexibility for their futures. Challenge yourself to go beyond their boundaries and break new ground. Choose a path that will cause your competitors to check their compass heading against yours. As you deliver your mission, they will reposition themselves to compete with you. By the time they catch up with you, you will have already moved on to the next adventure.

Approach diversification as if you were starting a new business. Develop a business plan independent from your existing operations and link the plan directly to your future competition in that particular industry. Compare the *Six Degrees* of the powerhouses in that industry to your *Six Degrees* in the same arena. Evaluate your ability to raise the necessary working capital, recruit the critical talent, and supply the required technology to start and support the new venture for the first five years. Then, take into account the risks and rewards to your existing revenue streams.

The next step is not for the weak. Design your end-game strategies before you make the first move. Just as one considers the necessary strategies for the last few rolls of the dice in backgammon or the final tricks in spades, take into account the end game moves for your new venture. Identify the strategies that will position you for success in the end and prepare a transitional plan for key leadership. From the beginning, take the time to select, mentor, and train your successors to ensure perpetuation of the mission.

Widen your appeal by narrowing your identity to what makes you distinctive. Chances are the current product or service you provide is also being sold by your competition. Question how the purpose of your product or service satisfies a need and creates a new market. When you prepare to deliver your new game, it is your culture and that of your colleagues, which makes the difference in cultivating and retaining new business. Ultimately, you will lead the market to a new future.

RESEARCH & DEVELOPMENT

The 3rd Degree

RESEARCH AND DEVELOPMENT

The 3rd Degree

Research and development captures the restless energy to seek new understanding and funnels it into achievement. However, R&D is a place where a great deal of financial and human resources are lost on an endless quest for information. The **Third Degree** looks at supplying R&D efforts with energy and focus which grants everyone in your organization a freedom of exploration permit.

Strong R&D positions you to make your product or service obsolete before the competition does it for you. Set the pace of progress and you will not only survive, but you will lead the marketplace. Surviving the path to success means understanding there are no ground rules. R&D is the survival kit for personal and professional success. If you are equipped with the proper gear, tools, compasses, and maps, you will discover new revenue, resources, and benchmarks for the competition to follow. When you change the formula in anticipation of changing needs, the market will move to keep up with you.

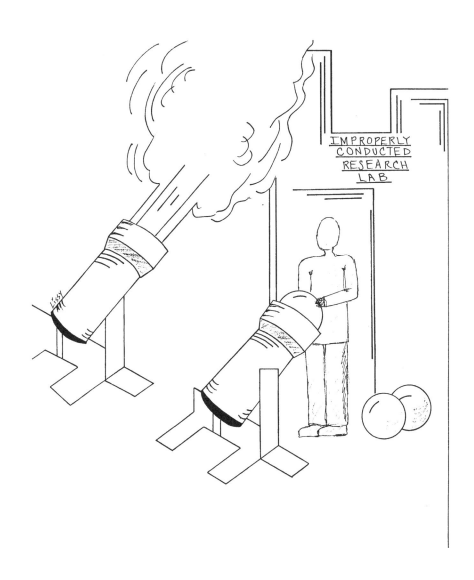

RESEARCH AND DESTROY

RESEARCH AND DESTROY

Military operations are known for their search and destroy tactics. Entire campaigns are built around the search and destroy principle of engagement. The parameters of a search and destroy mission are established through the use of intelligence reports needed to locate the enemy. Upon location of enemy forces, a strategic plan is created to vanquish the opponent.

Research and development provides the intelligence reports for a business campaign. If conducted improperly, it can become research and destruction instead of research and development. Most companies understand the need for research and development. However, they may lack the skills necessary to successfully build a research and development system.

We can handcuff our sales force if we fail to give them the necessary market intelligence to establish their advantage over the competition. A key component in strategic positioning is the thorough preparation of a research and development initiative. Prepare your R&D project for a new business campaign by evaluating the resources needed and risks taken in each of the *Six Degrees*. Constantly maintain focus on the long-term vision and desired outcomes for the campaign.

If the vision is shortsighted, the research and development initiative will be short-circuited.

The following steps can be used to facilitate your research and development process:

- Build a financial R&D commitment into your budget. Initially, even a small amount is sufficient.
- Work with local colleges and universities to enlist interns who can assist with the research and development infrastructure of your business.
- Establish an initial think tank session to capture any and all observations. These sessions will develop the framework for new opportunities.
- Compensate the team for the research and development initiatives producing profitable results.
- Discuss the research and development projects occurring at other organizations with your colleagues and friends. Often, you can become mutual partners in a project.
- Survey the marketplace and current clients to evaluate their future needs. This not only addresses client satisfaction, but also uncovers research and development issues.
- Solicit ideas from your co-workers. This expands your surface of potential opportunities and includes those who will be involved in their implementation.
- Review past failures because they can become the fabric for future research and development efforts.
- Establish a team of retired business masters. They have the skills and memory of their past experiences to assist with producing your future success.

Research and development should be managed as efficiently as a major expansion project. To ensure success, place consistent pressure on the follow-through and results of your R&D efforts. R&D success means never being beaten by an idea you should have had yourself.

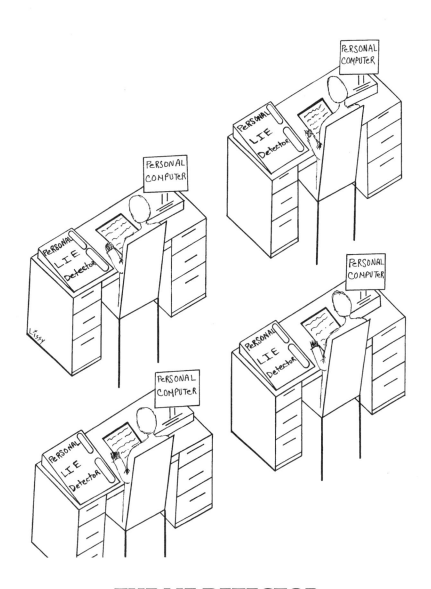

THE LIE DETECTOR

THE LIE DETECTOR

Imagine that you are hooked up to your own personal lie detector. It is better you know the results of your actions before the rest of the world has a chance to figure them out. We have a chance at the minimum sentence if we act as our own judge and jury. Let's visit the purpose of a personal lie detecting system.

A personal lie detector is a motivational grid plotting our true success. It has the ability to separate fact from fiction and reflects the image we project through the eyes of our audience.

We may be kidding ourselves about the amount of impact we create. If our performance were a pay-per-view event, would anyone order the show? If our absence goes unnoticed, there may be little reason to have a perpetuation plan set in place.

Life is a series of truth or dare scenarios. Since we may not always know when we are lying to ourselves, a personal lie detector is a truth or dare scenario. When you discover the truth about your own abilities, you can dare yourself to accomplish new challenges. Challenges that may have previously been viewed as lies.

We had a client who was struggling to implement a new management program. They were in the process of defining their corporate culture and internal management system. Within six months of the service contract, the insurance company wired the client to a lie detector test. In the opinion of the insurer, the client failed the test. Insurance claims were still on the rise and there did not appear to be any truth to the client's promises to change.

When we wired both parties to our lie detector, we determined both the insurer and the client were lying to themselves and to each other. The insurer did not believe they could generate enough impact to change the client's claim activity and the client did not believe they could retool their internal machinery to manage the claims.

The lie detector provides insight into our abilities to face challenge. It removes excuses and makes us answer to our true potential. Persistence then fills the gap between potential and performance. If we are consistent in meeting new challenges, we will be more than truthful about our performance.

THE GOAL DIGGERS

THE GOAL DIGGERS

There is no special dispensation granted to goal diggers. It is a trade they choose freely to counter their fear of being trapped in a mine with no challenges. There is no place in our minds that does not present opportunity. Never believe failure is an option and you will always strike goal as you wander through the darkness of above ground mines.

Some diggers worry about having properly staked their claim before reaching for their shovel and pick. They stop to read the posted signs before setting foot on a claim. The only claim you stake is the permission you grant yourself to deliver your peak performance. The history of past failures drives us to seek new solutions for the future. Staking claims serves to procrastinate initiative and limit opportunity. The only thing special about the goal digger's strategy is the persistence with which it is delivered.

Some people stake claims on their thoughts and ideas by shielding them in great secrecy. They believe the claim will protect them from competitors. However, there will always be claim jumpers robbing other's ideas to build their own fortune. Our ideas begin to age the moment they are born. Leaders who keep all of their secrets to themselves reek of insecurity and paranoia. Great leaders achieve multiple goals because they give away their secrets and place constant pressure on themselves to generate new concepts.

If you are relentless in designing and building your vision to look beyond the current mines you are excavating, you won't need to resort to claim jumping.

One of the best methods for creating focus in research and development expeditions is to put together a Dig Crew. The following strategies hold individuals accountable to themselves and each other:

♦ Bring the best diggers together through an initial high performance meeting to set the pace for the dig, establish each person's responsibility, and clarify the mission.
♦ Give them the permission to proceed and the forgiveness to fail at their best attempts.
♦ Enter the mine and guide the diggers on an excavation to travel without titles.
♦ Create an environment of mutual trust.
♦ Use all of your senses to find the cracks and crevices that provide opportunities for your clients.
♦ Deliver on expectations sooner than expected.
♦ Bring goals to a close with the entire crew.

Always remember to survey the prospects of your opportunities and avoid the flash of fool's goal. Charge your best talent with digging for every resource that will support striking your goals.

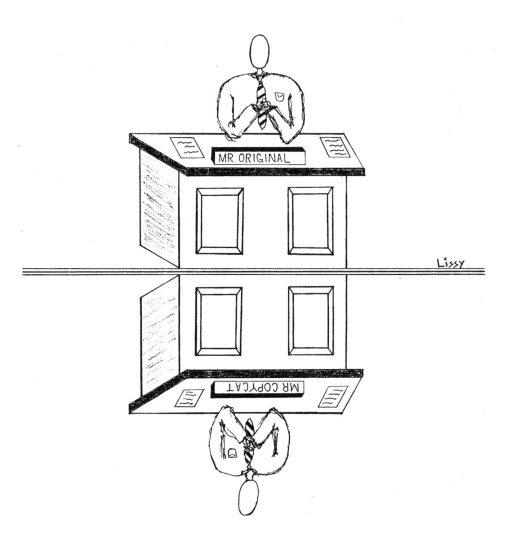

THE COPYCAT

THE COPYCAT

At the exact moment an idea is hatched, we are reminded the same discussion is probably occurring in at least three parallel universes as we see others are responding to the same environment and pressures in the marketplace. Odds are that predators will know about your idea well before you release it to the public. In many cases, they are likely to copy your work or improve upon it if possible.

Remember, you may see the future, but it is staring right back at you.

Anyone who believes they are the exception to this rule is in a state of denial. It is the nature of a copycat to live in a world filled with denial. Copycats may have a vision, but their duplicate style of originality often causes them to abandon their sense of urgency.

There are several telltale signs of copycats in denial. They may open their doors for business, but the client never shows. They became so impressed by the idea, they believe the dollars are sure to follow. When nothing appears, they believe the idea must have failed because of some factor out of their control.

If imitation is the sincerest form of flattery, being a copycat is the surest formula for failure. As the pressure to convert ideas into dollars is applied, copycats often get left in the dust. When the dust finally clears, they find themselves standing alone because they sacrificed creativity for process. A copycat won't be able to counter the creative cat's ability to deliver speed to market.

No one is immune to the copycat syndrome. To avoid falling into the copycat trap, we must focus new business development on opportunities that blend creativity with market speed. Never believe your own press and don't blame your shortcomings on your surroundings. Listen when your advisors complain about turf issues. Just because you can sell something doesn't mean it's a deal. Consider the reasons why people don't stay when there is a mass exodus of clients or colleagues occurring. Changing your strategy like it is the soup of the day won't make your product menu more exciting. Hold your need for change and speed accountable to your focus and direction.

When preparing to deliver a new product or service to the market, never allow the paranoia about piracy or concern for competition to shift your strategy from offense to defense. By the time the copycat has figured out how to duplicate your concept, you will already have moved on to the next project.

Remember you are a road warrior, not a road worrier. If you deliver your future with focus, all of the other cats will follow.

PRESSURE UNDER GLASS

PRESSURE UNDER GLASS

Imagine you are dining in one of the finest four-star restaurants in the world. You have just ordered pheasant under glass, the most expensive and highly recommended entrée on the menu. After an hour of patiently waiting, your server delivers to your table, with magnificent presentation, the pheasant under glass. You savor every bite and comment to your dining party that this has truly been the finest meal you have ever had.

At the same time, in a primitive hunting cabin, a hunter is preparing to eat his pheasant on an open fire with nothing more than a tree stump as a table. In place of the fine linen napkin you used, he has his shirtsleeve. After finishing his feast, he declares to his hunting buddies that this has truly been the greatest meal he has ever eaten.

Pheasant under glass doesn't taste any better than a pheasant eaten in the woods on a tree stump. When it comes to pressure, business professionals can fall into the same false impression as the restaurant patron. While working on a larger than normal deal, the pressure associated with it can taste differently and may create the sensation of having pressure served under glass. The moral of the story is that the presentation of pressure does not influence the degree of its impact.

Overachievers believe you can either eat your pressure under glass or barehanded with your fingers. They don't see pressure as a special item on the menu, but rather as part of their daily diet. They don't believe pressure comes in varying degrees. They can handle pressure either cold or fresh out of the oven. Regardless of the size of the problem they face, they are convinced inactivity creates negative pressure.

When dealing with pressure, never fear the problem but beware of the presentation. Overachievers don't let the presentation of the pressure intimidate them into inactivity. When you respond with action, the pressure is reduced to a solution.

Pressure appears more difficult when we place a problem under a glass lid and reduce activity. The inactivity presents pressure to appear larger than actual size when dealing with a more sophisticated problem. As with the story of the hunter, pheasant tastes like pheasant regardless of the presentation. Overachievers see pressure as the fuel to move past the presentation to the problem in search of the end result—the solution.

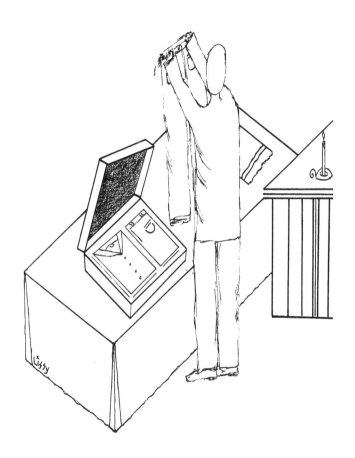

FADED GENES

FADED GENES

At the end of a long travel day, you arrive at your hotel room, unpack your flight bag, and remove the garment that immediately makes you relax — your favorite pair of faded jeans. As you put them on, you instantly feel calm. The long day of suits, heels, and ties is replaced with the beloved faded jeans. We can all relate to the comment, "I can't wait to get out of these clothes and put on a pair of jeans", which we often make to colleagues traveling with us after a long workday.

After a decade of heavy travel, it can feel like more than your jeans have faded. You imagine the biological genes that drove you to be a self-starting overachiever have begun to fade. Before the travel even starts, you begin to long for the trip home. You question whether or not you have the stamina to sustain the rigors of travel. The people at hotels and car rental lots know you by name. Restaurant servers around the country can place your order before you are seated.

Travelers hear everything and see nothing. Think about the nightly calls we make to our homes while traveling. The family takes turns on the phone sharing their experiences. We hear about their activities, but we rarely see them firsthand. We only see them happen in our imagination. Eventually, the genes fade and we become exhausted by the mere thought of the trip. There is little left in the flight bag to produce a calm at day's end.

There are ways to keep the genes jumping. Here are a few methods for staying energized and challenged. We cannot eliminate the stress of travel, but we sure can empathize and share our flight bag with you.

Whenever a new stress factor occurs, a new day begins. For example, your original flight has just been cancelled. You realize the meeting you have the next day begins at 7:00 am. You still have a two-hour drive to your hotel to look forward to when you arrive at your final destination. Estimated time of arrival is now 3:00 a.m. Focus your mind and body as though the day has just begun when you find yourself in a tight spot. The mind is your best tool to refresh your spirits and energize your body.

Never complain to those at home. They are powerless to change your situation and you'll only feel guilty about dumping on them later. Change the time in which you call home, so it becomes a welcomed surprise. If you can call more than once a day, make sure to do it. Children often miss their traveling parents more after the phone call ends.

Send postcards from the cities you visit. It goes a long way to connecting those at home with your line of sight. A travel journal will also assist you with maintaining energy and identifying success. Start a collection for the children. It will create a great educational and conversational connection. Remember to eat right and exercise. This sounds simple, but is often neglected. Work on a new challenge or project while on the road. A great deal of this book was written on the road.

Candles are a wonderful addition to your flight bag. They instantly alter the feeling of a hotel room by turning it into a warmer and more comfortable setting. Contact friends and colleagues living in the cities you visit. Sharing memories over dinner definitely helps to sooth the soul. If weekends at home mean religious celebrations, you should attend them while traveling. The theatre is a tremendous outlet for the solo traveler. Most cities have excellent troupes and the concierge at most hotels will produce tickets upon your request.

The genes can fade for those at home as well. The routine of daily life can be just as taxing as the trauma of travel. Whether in the hotel or the home, search for those techniques that can stimulate and energize you.

Pack your flight bag to combat any routine attempting to snare you.

The *Six Degrees of Impact* are only effective if you're healthy enough to deliver on your dreams. Travel is tough and the days can be rough. Try these tips and remember you are already a winner because you play a game where rules do not exist. Your genes will not fade and you will serve as a role model for others as their plane of life is cleared for takeoff.

MARKETING

The 4th Degree

MARKETING

The 4ᵗʰ Degree

Personal and organizational marketing are the key steps for attracting those who cross your path. So far, the focus of leadership and strategic positioning has been supported by research and development. In the *Fourth Degree,* we develop strategies for internal and external marketing. Marketing pulls together the first three degrees to deliver an image and focus which transcends any brochure or website.

We have always believed a critical aspect of marketing is the speed at which an organization delivers a new product to the marketplace. The same theory applies to the marketing going on within an organization. Human and technological energy converts plans into action. The results you have achieved in your performance outcomes are ready to be broadcast.

TEN SECONDS TO IMPACT

TEN SECONDS TO IMPACT

Often times it seems we only have ten seconds to make an impression. In our professional environments, we meet people and rarely discuss anything except the business aspect of the relationship. Constant demands and an intense sense of urgency have left us little time to develop the humanity in business. In reality, our business will become more successful if we take the time necessary to make a better impression on people.

The humanity of business is the most important aspect of building our professional relationships. It is impossible to understand the client's needs without an understanding of the client.

Contrary to the opinion of many business leaders, profit is not the primary motive of business. Without dedicated clients, there is no potential for profit. Impact that leaves a positive impression must be our first priority. Contact is not the same as impact. In our careers, we may encounter dozens of contacts and never make a single solid impact.

Without delivering a memory-denting impact, we will have difficulty cultivating a contact. Over the years, we have attended many national conferences as both presenters and exhibitors. The professionals who score conference success based on the number of business cards they have acquired have been a great source of comic relief for us. We have seen contact systems ranging from door prizes to cocktail receptions. Although numerous contacts were made, very few memory-denting impacts actually occurred.

Most fail to realize that only a few impacts are needed to develop true client prospects. It is the memory-denting impacts that will later build successful client referrals. When we are constantly pitching our product and service, we forget to listen to others. Listening builds the foundation of impact when needs are heard and solutions can be developed.

Mr. Carl Conference is the perfect example of a contact player. Mr. Conference was standing in the middle of a reception at a large national convention. Mr. Conference was great at approaching people at the party because he was a natural cold-caller. Every time Carl would engage someone in conversation, his eyes would be focused on his next "contact" in the crowd. After the reception, Carl showed us the bundle of business cards he had amassed. Although Carl's contact system may have developed volume, it lacked impact. We later learned that many people gave Carl their cards so he would leave them alone. His lack of sincerity was evident when everyone sensed Carl's poor focus and concentration.

There are keys to developing the skill of impact. View every environment as the impact playing field and know you only have seconds to make an impression. Professional desperation is easy to spot and there is no place for desperation in the personality of the professional. Do not push your agenda on anyone. Listen to the issues and make observations that match the needs of the client to your skill package. A skill package encompasses both your personal skills and those of your company. Never treat people as scores on your prospect game sheet and never send personnel who are weak at creating impact to build client contacts.

Every handshake is a chance to impact. The greatest client service systems are rendered useless without the foundation of impact players.

Impact players have the ability to focus in an extremely active environment. They are the ultimate listeners because they genuinely care about the people they meet. Success will follow you when you take the time to make an impact. Remember you have ten seconds to impact, so check your systems and be prepared to encounter your future friend and client.

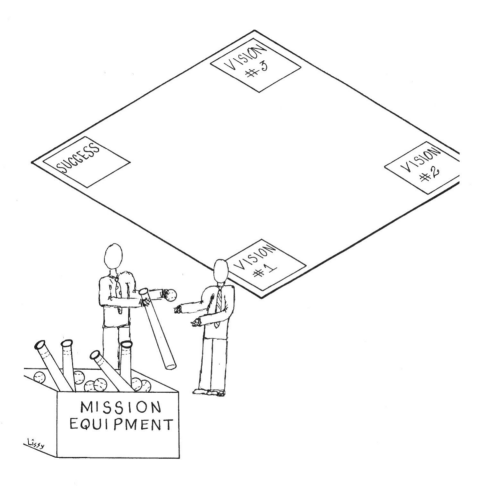

TELLING ISN'T SELLING

TELLING ISN'T SELLING

Most of us haven't developed the psychic powers necessary to understand what is expected of us without it being communicated. Given this limitation, the responsibility to communicate and teach falls back on the leader. Many professionals make the mistake of thinking telling qualifies as selling. Often times, they believe colleagues will be instinctively motivated and sold on an idea simply because they are told what needs to be done.

One manager was ineffective at assigning tasks to people and prevented them from having total ownership of projects. Anyone found working contrary to his methods was removed from the project. The second person assigned was given explicit details. As a result, they were successful, while their colleague was charged with failure. In the end, the first person was set up to fail and stripped of their motivation to achieve on future projects.

Surprisingly, many still believe we can eliminate managing or motivating colleagues if we have the right personnel. This belief throws all responsibility for performance outcomes back to the individual and allows the leader to discard the role of coach and mentor. We have seen leaders who took this responsibility to the extreme. In one case, an executive decided to make hiring decisions based on a coin toss, eliminating the need for screening, training, or managing people.

We must always remember telling is not teaching. People are more inclined to operate effectively when you offer valuable feedback. Consider the view from their perspective. If we don't understand the methodology, we are more likely to create shortcuts. As leaders, we must step up to the role of coach and mentor to equip each player with a mission.

Every successful product has a vision. People buy it because they are sold on how well it will perform. The product of vision is sold when the buyer can imagine the view.

Take time to review your objectives. Anticipate obstacles and never dwell on the agony of defeat. Focus discussion on the impact decisions will have on the future. Discuss solutions and forecast the benefits of success to everyone involved. Answer why you would step up to the task and be prepared to sell the vision. When you illustrate the vision, others will make the climb and share the view with you.

AD-VENTURE PLANNING

AD-VENTURE PLANNING

We are all bombarded by hundreds of ways to spend our money and place business. The competition for the public's attention and dollars is fierce. Marketing campaigns never suffer from being too interesting. They are sure to have elements of ad-venture no matter which successful marketing formulas were used. Ad-venture marketing distinguishes your campaign from the competition and earns consideration from your prospects.

The first step in planning an ad-venture marketing campaign is learning about conditions in the environment. Like introducing a new species into an ecosystem, everything from weather to predators will determine the product's chances for survival. Before you start building a marketing plan, take the time to review changes in the marketplace, assess your client base, determine the players, and anticipate any cost shifts which may occur. These factors will uncover potential threats to success and determine the strength of your focus.

When evaluating new ventures, consider problems as opportunities for impact. A businessman approached us with a dream for developing a new product. He had the dream for years, but never pursued it because others had discouraged him. They believed his idea would be unsuccessful because it was designed for an underprivileged market that couldn't afford to buy the product. When he described the dream, we saw the potential because it offered ad-venture. The market which had been perceived as a limitation actually presented an opportunity for others who were invested in the same vision. Due to strong public opinion and positive image, his dream came true and became the reality for others.

The promises of an ad-venture must be built on a solid image to reach the summit of sale. If we build image on true character rather than the flaws of others, a solid reputation will follow. Share the opportunities you offer and communicate your beliefs. Advertising will insure more people see the image you create. If the product is flawed, advertising will make certain the marketplace knows you have an inferior product.

When a client joins you on an ad-venture, you are linked in a joint venture for mutual success. It is the efforts of the climbing party and the guides who will determine the success of the expedition.

Clients will embark on your ad-venture not because the campaign looks good, but because they know you are committed to guiding them to their summit.

Leverage your position to help your clients reach the next base camp. Contrast character and capabilities with your competitors to define the business climate. Identify strategic markets that will build reputation for anyone associated with the expedition. A great ad-venture will give the client additional skills in their survival pack to reach their summit.

SELLING INSIDE-OUT

SELLING INSIDE-OUT

Ultimately, our survival depends upon our ability to deliver services through an integrated system built by both the client and supplier. Selling inside-out promotes passion for the project and reduces corporate paranoia. Corporate paranoia ensues because the client has been led to believe the supplier is seeking an unfair advantage. Selling inside-out reduces the paranoia by establishing a partnership at the time of proposal development.

If we break down the moves for selling inside-out, it begins with leaving preconceptions at the door. Sometimes, it is simplified by selling to someone you know on the inside or leaving behind brochures and media kits. However, it is much more. It is about being real. Learn about your prospective client by watching and listening for their genuine needs. If we consider our clients as humans rather than targets, we become partners rather than predators. Instead of wasting their time, we should take the time to learn more about them.

A successful marketer is the extreme corporate clinician.

Diagnose the problem, identify the need, and match up the resources. When maximizing outcomes for your clients is your primary concern, they will realize meaningful results. Whether or not this becomes significant to anyone else in the market will depend on how successful your results are with your current clients. If the treatment results in increased independence and success, others will seek the same.

Individuals who sell from the inside-out attack needs with drive and passion. For them, it is never a game of easy come and easy go. They are able to see new opportunities even on their worst day. On the other hand, most marketers present their proposal on their corporate stationary. This is commonplace, predictable, and totally outside selling. Instead, try using your corporate clinical skills to assess the client's individual needs and deliver the proposal in their language and on their letterhead. When you prepare the final product in partnership with the client, the energy invested results in a product serving the real needs of both parties. Create an internal selling conduit with a greater chance for success in closing the deal and delivering results by implementing the following steps:

♦ Leave your preconceptions at the door
♦ Listen, watch, and learn about their *Six Degrees*
♦ Break down the needs of your clients
♦ Remember where there is smoke, there are people gasping for air, so help them to get out safely
♦ Work all your resources to help them reach their dreams

Inside-out selling is built on a foundation established by both parties. In construction, the general contractor meets with all of the subcontractors to establish job parameters. If we apply this to business, we can achieve the *Six Degrees of Impact,* the integration of systems and professionals focused on a common goal.

THE HUMAN APPARITION

THE HUMAN APPARITION

There is the human spirit and then there is human nature. We had an experience leaving us with a sad comment on both. We met a human whose spirit was transformed from a motivated life force into a human apparition right before our eyes.

She was a young woman who agreed to embark on a project with us. She had shown the excitement and commitment we look for when selecting partners in any endeavor. We signed the contract and began to plan our strategy. After some changes, we realized the partnership would produce greater results if we delayed the start date by a few weeks. When we presented her with the need for adjustment, the necessary change evoked an unfortunate and disappointing response from her. Her human spirit had turned into a human apparition. Her commitment to the project became vague and transparent. She demanded payment in guilt and fees for the personal torment she perceived the change had caused her.

The human apparition chooses personal torment over personal commitment, eventually sacrificing the ambitions of their colleagues in fear of trust.

It was clear we were not the first clients on which her spirit had faded. Her drive and motivation to deliver a premium product had faded at the first light of difficulty. She had lost sight of her own mission to support her clients in achieving their dreams. So many had misrepresented themselves to her in the past that she expected failure now. Legal proceedings and pressure tactics had become a way of doing business and had distracted her focus from the objective.

We all have a limited number of resources we can dedicate to living our personal and professional lives. Maintaining flexibility in both is critical to meeting the needs of our families and our businesses. Protect the motivation of your human spirit by setting clear expectations for every endeavor. Prepare yourself for the best and the worst case scenarios and never allow change to deliver disappointment or anger. Find the advantage for yourself and you will also find it for your clients.

People will adapt to meet a challenge if their spirit is rewarded with opportunity. Confidence in one's ability to deliver on a goal makes legal crowbars and pressure tactics seem like useless tools. The spirit triumphs when the reward is drawn from achievement.

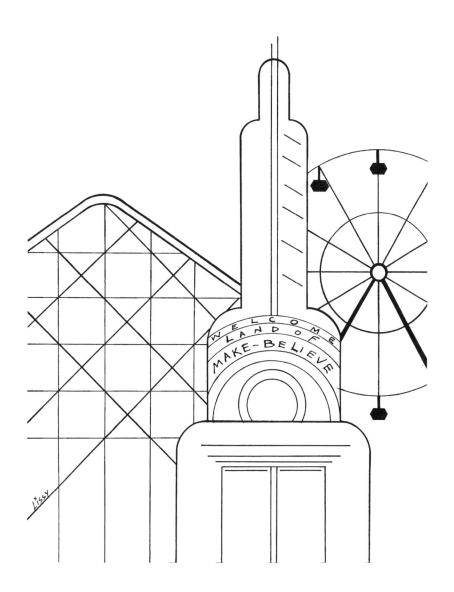

THE LAND OF MAKE-BELIEVERS

THE LAND OF MAKE-BELIEVERS

The illusionist can make you believe the impossible by performing magic right in front of your eyes. With only a slight of hand, the card you selected appears at the top of the deck. Leaders have the same ability. They can make an organization appear on top of the marketplace with only a few positive words and minimal contact. Leaders live in the Land of Make-Believers, where illusion turns impossibility into reality.

The illusionist is the ultimate marketer of the future. They are always searching for opportunities to perform the impossible.

Every day, we are confronted with situations requiring us to make choices. The only real dilemma in decision-making is the choice between solutions and opportunities. Beware of limiting your focus to finding the solution to solve a particular problem. It can narrow your thinking to fixing a singular situation and creates a danger zone of impossibility. You will soon find yourself trapped in a mystery with nothing but questions in sight.

Looking for the "right" answer can limit your opportunity. Choose to seek out opportunity at every impasse and you will overcome impossibility to find the advantage in any predicament. If you stretch your imagination, you will no longer need to travel the roads of process in search of the perfect answer. After overcoming impossibility, you will find any decision you make to be the right one.

The illusionist understands there is not just one "right" answer to any question. If you keep your eye on opportunity, the future will always bring advantage into focus. Conquer the impossible by using predictable moments to create surprising results. For instance, many believe it is impossible to lead an organization without physically being present to reinforce leadership and set performance standards. If someone can travel the world in their minds from a rocking chair on their porch, then a leader can travel the minds of their leadership crew and look them in the eye without standing in the same room. Create the illusionist's trapeze by giving people the sense of movement without taking one step. Keep yourself in view of others by contacting them at least weekly, help them find opportunities, and listen for how you can help them succeed.

When you realize you can travel anywhere from where you stand, the impossible will become probable. Lead your colleagues to the Land of Make-Believers and you will create magic through invention and opportunity. Invite everyone to stretch their imagination to perform their ultimate illusion and you will turn an unproductive workforce into a motivated crew. Show confidence and faith in your markets and they will return business to you as you deliver the ultimate illusion…reality.

HUMAN RESOURCES

The 5th Degree

HUMAN RESOURCES

The 5ᵗʰ Degree

There is no resource more valuable to an organization than its colleagues. Anyone can deliver your product, but no one can duplicate your performance. It is the dedication and commitment of each individual to achieving their personal best, allowing organizations to become leaders.

In the *Fifth Degree*, we focus on how to support the development of personal and professional skills, enabling consistent and powerful performance in any arena. Mentoring colleagues to understand the strategic plan and encouraging them to contribute their individual assets builds a persistent force charged with the energy to carry out the mission.

TURNABOUT IS FAIR PLAY

TURNABOUT IS FAIR PLAY

As long as we can remember, employment relationships have been based on the employee working for the employer or owner. The employee was eager to hang onto a job because good jobs were hard to find. Employers were in the catbird's seat and could hire the pick of the litter.

Today, the tables have certainly turned. We hear employers in every industry speak of their frustration in recruiting and retaining a qualified and talented workforce. If you look across an interview desk today, you are likely to find the candidate asking the tough questions while the employer hopes they have the right answers.

The "employee" is the owner of their own company and the organization is the candidate applying for their "human" resources.

This trend is only expected to continue. As service industries continue to grow and technology makes our lives less complicated or at least different, available jobs will outnumber the working population. "Employees" will shrink in numbers and organizations will draw talent from a pool of independents. Skill packages will evolve from multi-tasking on one job to multi-jobbing one task or skill. People will work less structured hours and offices will exist in cyberspace.

Consider the changing demands facing the working population. As employers scramble to become more competitive in their strategies to recruit talent, designing creative benefit packages has become critical in attracting talent to your resource pool. Employers of choice will offer the benefits of independence and ownership with the support of a small community. Build your organization's employer resumé and develop the following benefits to attract talent to your organization:

♦ Provide Life-Balance services. Offer guidance to colleagues on managing life events such as parenting, dealing with medical crises, or caring for an aging loved one. Every year, increased productivity is lost as an aging work force directs their focus towards caring for aging family members. Support your colleagues during these life transitions.

♦ Design mentoring programs fitting your culture. Many organizations implement cookie cutter models without providing the pace needed to challenge an individual's growth. Offer mentoring which provides realistic growth opportunities, shortens job life spans, and strengthens perpetuation.

♦ Coordinate the telecommunications frenzy. Since the speed of technological change is already exceeding the speed limit in most people's minds, determine their needs and maximize their communications power as simply as possible. Value quality people with quality equipment. The more you can eliminate the fray, the more inclined colleagues are to stay.

Ultimately, it comes down to the bottom line. However, this bottom line is evaluated by the independent, which expects the investment of their personal resources to produce financial, intellectual, and social returns. Employers who can successfully turnabout their employment mindset will realize human resources are essential for gaining the competitive edge in the marketplace.

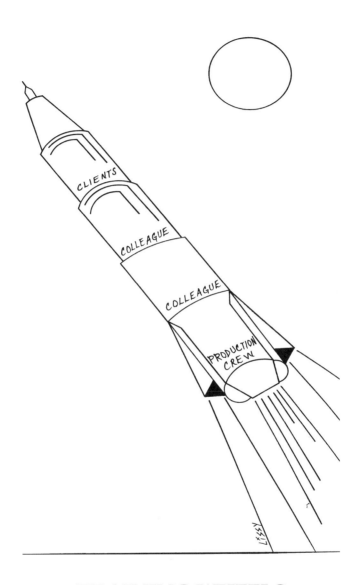

TRAINING WHEELS

TRAINING WHEELS

Corporate titles are like permanent training wheels. They limit the focus of an individual's learning to one vehicle. If we are forced to chose titles for our colleagues, the only title should be producer. Regardless of our role, producer delivers the most effective definition. Traditionally, a producer is the one responsible for sales and marketing. No organization can survive without new business and client retention. Consider all colleagues as producers. From the corner office to the mailroom, we are all members of the production crew serving the client.

Most organizational charts only list the leadership team members. Our organizational chart is a graphic of the space shuttle in which the cockpit contains our clients. The balance of the shuttle holds the "production crew" and lists every colleague by name. Our flight mission is to transport our clients to success. Our chart is informative and motivational. Informative because it states mission and vision. Motivational because everyone sees they are important in achieving successful organizational results.

Titles are like organizational training wheels. The longer they remain on the organization, the tougher it becomes to balance the roles and responsibilities creating new production.

Intense and focused training systems are an important method for installing creativity and consistent performance. We constantly witness boring and ineffective training programs. The absence of cross training is the birth of colleague turnover and the death of marketing. They concentrate on titles, texts and certificates versus people, productivity and retention.

The following twelve guidelines will assist you with establishing an innovative training system:

- Be sure all training has marketing and retention as the ultimate goal
- Involve all colleagues in training opportunities
- Use the training program to develop presentation skills
- Link all training programs to long- range planning goals
- Review trainer performance with evaluation forms similar to those used at educational seminars
- Promote fieldwork to increase direct communication with clients
- Use case studies of actual client situations
- Build training curriculums with outlines and performance objectives
- Invite clients to join cooperative training sessions
- Encourage study groups for internal work projects
- Allow different colleagues to present at board and management meetings
- Encourage leadership to train alongside other colleagues

In your organization, try to build a training system founded on the producer principle. View everyone as a producer who contributes to the organization's ultimate success. Remove the training wheels and pedal to productivity. When a fall occurs, jump back on and ride to your goals.

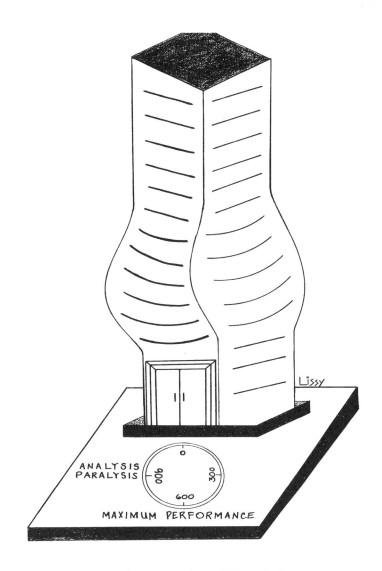

WAIT WATCHERS

WAIT WATCHERS

One of the greatest challenges an individual or business must face is managing wait. To maintain your optimal wait, you have to achieve a balanced diet of process and results along with a high-impact exercise program.

Many organizations suffer from a wait problem. Over-wait businesses allow people to process routine as the optimal method of operations. Their diet consists of multiple forms and meetings they consume in excess when facing competition. Eventually, they suffer from analysis paralysis by allowing the routine to drive the decision-making process. Under-wait businesses have cut all of the process from their diet and make many of their decisions without the minimum daily information requirement. A balanced diet combines the necessary process with a focus on results to achieve maximum performance.

To survive the challenge of competition, every member of an organization must reach a high level of involvement and accomplishment. Consider every moment as an opportunity to get closer to your goal. Whether you reach the goal or not depends on persistence — *your* persistence to fill the gap between potential and performance.

The performance goals you set will measure your progress and recognize your achievements. Responsibility to the goal and accountability to quality should be your guides to managing resources. When you attend a meeting, think about the cost to your business. Weigh the meeting's productivity against the personnel costs invested. Evaluate how today's actions will impact tomorrow's goal.   Think about your time investments and develop a profit and loss statement that includes revenues, expenses, and the bottom line. When you talk to people, take into consideration how your interaction with them will impact on profit. You can decide to make a charitable contribution to a non-profit, but be sure to record your gift credit.

Contributions of time and energy should only be made for one of two reasons: compensation or satisfaction.

Take the time to look in the performance mirror and step on the outcome scale to see your results. Eventually, you will become more motivated to take on a rigorous training schedule. Your focus will shift from simply performing routine exercises and eating frozen diet meals to targeted body shaping and endurance building. Instead of attending a committee meeting like it was an exercise class that didn't require much effort, establish an individualized training program with specific goals. Set performance targets for your strategic plan, market development, client base, prospect hunts, and service delivery. Monitor progress to review internal and external factors like change, responses, surprises, and improvements.

Equipped with persistence, goals, and a training program, the place where you are now will become the place you are coming from tomorrow. As you turn back to look at your progress, you will only see the potential of the future. Watch your wait, pack your persistence, and go!

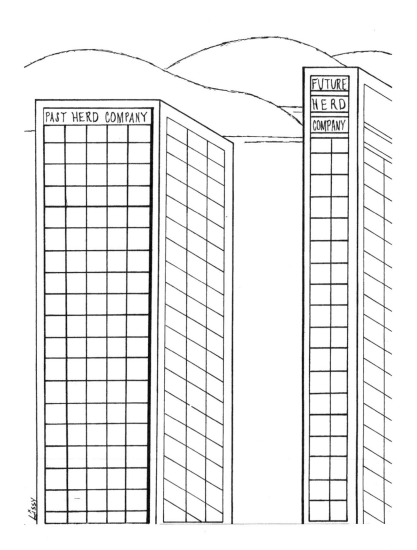

THINNING THE HERD

THINNING THE HERD

The theory of natural selection is just as critical for business survival as it is in nature. Thinning the herd controls over-population and selects the stronger individuals for positions of growth to insure the survival and success of the group. Every business faces the threat of natural predators who sense weakness and move in for the kill. It is our overachievers who challenge potential and push performance to the next level.

We owe it to the overachievers to choose evolution over extinction. Thinning the herd prompts us all to adapt our skills for survival.

During a strategic planning session with a non-profit organization, the group reached a conflict during perpetuation planning. They realized they would have to select certain individuals for fast-track mentoring. We had suggested an effective method for thinning the herd.

Initially, identifying people with the talent and drive necessary to mentor the next generation seemed like discrimination to this group. Soon, they realized their business environment would select them for extinction if they did not take the steps necessary to mentor the leaders and thinkers of their organization.

Influential organizations have influential leaders. Encourage the leaders and thinkers of your organization to re-invent themselves through personal remodeling. An organization adapts quickly to market shifts when the leaders measure their results against others, shape the quality of their delivery to respond to the environment, and mentor the motivated.

If change is for everybody, then evolution is for the motivated.

Consider the hard chargers you know. They strive to adapt to new environments and follow their impulse for progress. We can spot them using all of their senses to aim for maximum impact. They see the vision of the future, hear problems as opportunities, smell the scent of strategy, touch souls with sincerity, and know the taste of humility. If we mentor their future, the unlimited growth of our peers will follow.

ITS SO NICE TO MEET YOU !

THE DISEASE OF INDIFFERENCE

THE DISEASE OF INDIFFERENCE

In today's constantly changing business arena, technology is necessary to successfully compete and excel. The mere rumor of a computer virus can send us into a death spiral to secure invisible data. Despite this, the most deadly of the viruses striking individuals or organizations is not a computer virus. It is the disease of indifference. This disease is usually characterized by shifting blame, deflecting responsibility, or lack of concern. Regardless of how the disease manifests itself, it results in disregard for others and focuses on the survival of one individual — the carrier.

On more than one occasion, we have seen cultures where leadership was not motivated to invest in the success of the organization. While some had grown tired of the battle against the fear of change and hid in their foxholes to avoid confrontation, others believed they were en"title"d to early job retirement and joined the office putt-putt tour. Unfortunately, the disease of indifference is often contagious.

The only antidote for the disease of indifference is the passion to perform. We have to compete against the best and stop whining with the rest.

To fight the disease, one must maintain their personal wellness program, exercise high-impact time management, take daily challenges, and control their whine intake. Run the corporate obstacle course with an eye for opportunity. Maintain a strong posture for personal accountability and you will improve your own fitness as well as the health of those around you.

The disease of indifference causes some professionals to resist building friendships with clients and colleagues because they fear eventually finding themselves in a compromising situation. They believe personal commitments demand a bond that forgives poor performance and requires a blind eye. To the contrary, true personal commitment calls for honest feedback and individual accountability.

The best prevention for the disease of indifference is personal accountability. At a young age, we both learned accountability because we knew even our own mothers would fire us if we were found slacking on the job. Commitment to our colleagues increases our responsibility to deliver our best professional performance. It is a promise to honor obligations without compromise. The disease of indifference has no chance of infecting us if we exercise interest, respect, and understanding.

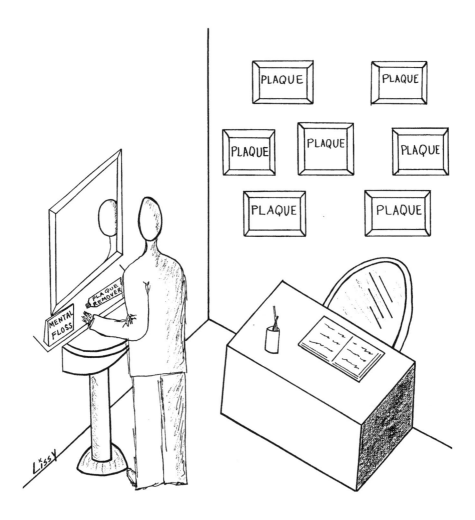

ULTIMATE PLAQUE REMOVAL SYSTEM

ULTIMATE PLAQUE REMOVAL SYSTEM

Often times, the recipient of a professional award can have terrible plaque build-up. Most of us have seen the "walls of greatness" which accumulate from years of recognition and achievement. We know plaque build-up is occurring when the plaques on the wall begin to take up more square footage than the wallpaper. If we allow plaque build-up to occur, it can tarnish the smile of accomplishment with smugness.

The ultimate plaque remover is to scrape the plaque off your own smile and place it on the smile of your colleagues.

Think about the executive who has received more plaques than wall space to hang them on. Although they are presented with appreciation and accepted with gratitude, the single name engraved is usually one of several who contributed to the success. Some leaders are inclined to bring the trophies back to camp and quietly store them away. Others may chose to display their achievements on the wall. The ceremonial rebel may hang their diplomas upside-down and put Chiquita banana stickers on them to protest the pomp of degrees and titles. Regardless of where we hang our plaques, it is where we place the smile they bring which ultimately prevents plaque build-up.

When you receive an award, recognize the achievement of your colleagues who contributed to the success by asking them to sign it. This creates a personally engraved plaque that you can all wear with pride. There is no limit to what we can accomplish if we don't care who gets the credit. If we eliminate plaque build-up, our smiles will be more contagious.

Another method for eliminating your plaque build-up is with the smiles that worked to achieve the goals. Take all of the plaques off of your walls and replace them with pictures of friends and colleagues who supported you in building your character and reputation. Their smiles leave lasting recognition of the dreams you accomplished together.

To prevent future plaque build-up, you should remember to use mental floss regularly. When we dedicate ourselves to proper motivational hygiene, momentum comes from the pace of accomplishment rather than the flash of recognition. If we fail to realize the tentative nature of success and glare at achievement too long, we will lose our balance and fall. The smile of accomplishment creates confidence in the ability to achieve and becomes recognition for everyone's efforts.

FAKING IT ISN'T GOOD FOR ANYBODY

FAKING IT ISN'T GOOD FOR ANYBODY

People tend to respond in one of two ways when confronted with performing a task outside of their skill package. They either ask for help or they fake it.

Faking it can be hazardous to your health. If you step into the boxing ring without any lessons, you will ultimately feel your face against the mat.

One ineffective training approach is partnering a rookie with an experienced fighter who has a great performance record, but no teaching skills. The rookie tries to pick up skills by shadowing the more experienced professional. The result leaves the rookie with critical gaps in what they actually learn. They may develop into a championship shadow boxer, but they never learn how to land a punch. Without learning technique and strategy, the rookie has no chance of being a contender. In time, the rookie becomes too embarrassed to admit their lack of skills and will attempt to survive as many rounds as possible by faking it. Shadowing without mentoring is the fast track to losing new talent.

Look at training and education as you would look at planning a nutritional program for a championship fighter. The less specific the regimen, the harder it is to establish consistent health and reliable performance. If you don't understand their physical needs and pretend to know what you're recommending, they are likely to show inconsistent technique and poor stamina.

Take the time to train the trainer on how to break strategies down into techniques and match the lessons up with an individual's reference points. Speed of learning is a function of our ability to connect new skills with old habits. Consistent performance results from persistence and practice.

To evaluate progress, simply look, listen, and learn. Ask the rookie to explain how they would respond to specific situations. In doing this, you will discover whether or not you have missed an exercise in practice and determine if more sparring may be needed. When trying to convince a rookie to use your methods, be willing to take some of the hits to keep them off of the ropes. Adjust the strategies to maximize their instinctual responses. The ultimate knockout punch is a combination of practice, technique, and natural instinct. Regardless of the weight class, the rewards of earning a true victory will always outweigh the reasons for faking it.

CORPORATE GRAVE ROBBERS

CORPORATE GRAVE ROBBERS

Corporate grave robbers are business people who constantly allow the past to dictate the present. They view change through the yellowed lens of the past. Although it is always important to learn from past experiences, trouble begins when we freeze present opportunity to mourn the past.

Corporate grave robbers fear the light of change. They work best in the darkness of past glories. They find it easier to dig up old victories than to create new challenges.

Corporate grave robbers are usually found in small groups. They require the aid of the group to lift the coffins of corporate cadavers. When a visionary begins to see the future, you can be sure the grave robbers are preparing to raise a dead ideal. They will attempt to crush the future challenge by comparing it to a deceased legend of the past. They are skilled at resurrecting the obituary written to honor a past achievement.

We had the opportunity to stumble upon an actual corporate grave robbing in progress. Three grave robbers were conducting new colleague orientation. One of the trainees had a new marketing idea and asked one of the grave robbers if the marketing department would consider their concept. Cleverly disguised as a trainer, the grave robber uncovered a grave and stated the following obituary: "Several years ago, our prior sales manager had the same idea. He tried desperately to implement a marketing plan similar to the one you have suggested. After several months, our sales manager realized the market would never respond to such a campaign. I appreciate your idea, but it was tried before." After hearing the trainer's response, the new colleague lowered her head. An appropriate response considering that she was standing at a corporate gravesite.

We knew the sales manager the corporate grave robber spoke of and we can honestly say he never had the idea presented by the new sales person. Today, the trainer is no longer with the organization and the former trainee is a top producer. We should never allow the ghosts of the past to scare away the visionaries of the future.

There are times when a walk down memory lane is therapeutic. When leaders need a lift, the past victories and corporate storytelling can provide a revitalizing tonic. The system begins to break down when the past becomes our only roadmap to the future. Maps can become outdated and force us to make wrong turns, causing us to become lost.

Respect the memory of your past achievements. Buy flowers on the anniversary of their passing. Remember the challenges of the future are the charities requiring our leadership contribution. Charge ahead to your goals and achievements. While corporate grave robbers use shovels to dig downward, visionaries use ladders to climb upward.

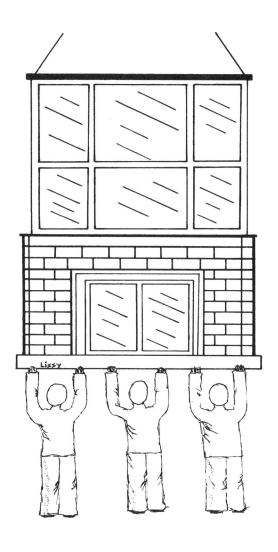

MENTAL MANAGEMENT

MENTAL MANAGEMENT

The one survival characteristic every leader seeks is the ability to sense change in their environment. Leadership requires the instinct to act on what you hear, smell, see, and feel. Most leaders don't fail because they lack intelligence or understanding for their business, but because they sensed a problem and ignored all of the warning signs.

In most cases, the management structure they depended on failed and caused irreparable stress cracks. All of the pressure was coming to bear on one square inch, a few overachievers. We suggest replacing the inflexibility of a traditional middle management with a strong "mental" management structure, able to contract and expand to meet environmental pressures.

The misguided allegiances of a leader may threaten the strength of an organization. For some, it may be blind or personal commitment to their draft pick. Others may believe they can coach anyone to succeed if given enough time. Many choose to work with the devil they know instead of the devil they don't know. Regardless of their motivation, leaders no longer have the luxury of avoiding the bad press of firing a long-time colleague or donating the majority of their time to developing weak management potential. When colleagues are caught running short of their goals, leaders must make the call to change the line up and place people in other positions that encourage their peak performance.

If you take time to consider the differences between two companies peddling the same products with only one being successful, you will usually find the one critical difference between the two is their people.

Place people first, strategy second, and success will follow. People are the reinforcing rods of every organizational structure.

Replace middle management conflicts with the strength of a mental management structure. Wipe out the top, middle, and other muddled layers of management. Create a mental management structure that places equal pressure where everyone stands and reduces the risk of stress cracks. Develop a system valuing everyone's contribution to the organization's production and delivery. Build on the greatest natural resource that delivers a championship performance of your strategic plan...your human resources.

Begin by devoting time and energy to learning the individual goals and dreams of the leaders around you. Evaluate colleagues by their *Six Degrees of Impact* and allow everyone to gain a 360-degree perspective on their performance through honest feedback. If you fix individual performance leaks, the efficiency of production will follow. Leadership is not just about building relationships, but also about building confidence. Every day is a journey on which we must support each other in reaching our destinations. With a full mental management structure in place, everyone becomes responsible for sensing the changes in the environment and players will strive to improve their game.

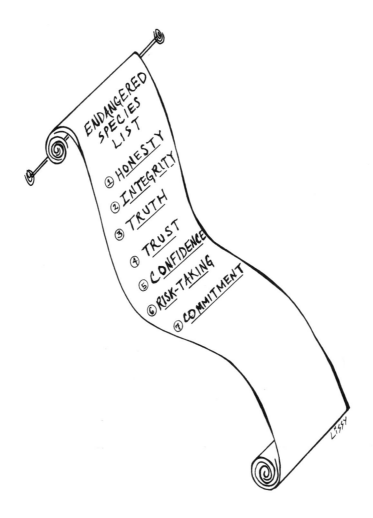

HONESTY: THE ENDANGERED SPECIES

HONESTY: THE ENDANGERED SPECIES

In today's workplace, honesty is an endangered species. Even when you think you have spotted it, you may reach out to touch it and discover someone's integrity has disappeared into extinction right before your eyes.

There is really only one reason why people avoid the truth. It is survival. The 'flight or fight response' leads the mind to question a person's own actions and answer their fears. It may be the fear of making a mistake that makes history or the fear of standing for something when others will not. The fear can also be of losing ground and losing face. Suddenly, fear builds into an accumulation of half-truths appearing more viable than the truth. Half-truths rob opportunity of the ability to deliver trust.

Only trust will remove fear and replace doubt with confidence and performance. When we sacrifice honest feedback, we rob others of the opportunity to set new personal goals. Often times, this can be seen when unsatisfactory performance is recognized, but not confronted until someone is suddenly moved or terminated. The blow of an unsuspected and sudden consequence usually leaves the victim with the "deer in the headlights" look. They never realized they should have tried to do something differently. Individuals who fail to confront others with honest feedback are not leaders, but cheaters. They frequently sacrifice commitment to their colleagues to install a quick fix or serve their own personal agendas.

In the end, the choice for anything less than integrity leaves nothing more than face value. Eventually, predators will sense you are no real threat and put you on the endangered species list.

Think of your company as an ecosystem requiring a balance of life forms to insure survival and growth. One of the greatest threats to an organization's ecosystem is the absence of trust. Consider the energy you see devoted to spreading criticism and disappointment in others on any given day. Listen and be honest about what you hear. If you replace criticism and disappointment with support and solutions, you will create an environment focused on evolution rather than the threat of its predators.

Build an environment of trust and growth. We can expect people to take chances on learning only if we give them the space to explore their skills. Teach individuals to grant themselves permission to make mistakes. Help others to pursue their dreams and don't criticize the risk they are willing to take. In areas where others have failed, they may succeed.

If leaders find a colleague facing unmet expectations, they must help them stand up with dignity and move forward. The pressure of disappointment which overachievers place on themselves is always greater than the pressure anyone else can put on them. Choose to broker in honesty rather than disappointment and colleagues will seek your counsel. If failure occurs because a commitment was made but no energy was invested, the leader is responsible for delivering pressure to create focus.

If we are honest with ourselves, failure will never be unknown or sudden. It is everyone's responsibility to design survival or end-game strategies when others fail. End-game strategies will prepare you to pull out the survivors and execute the alternatives. Teach everyone to think about turning losses into opportunities. If you focus energy on helping each other meet the overall bottom line, you will strengthen your position in the marketplace and your ability to fight competition. Invest in integrity and you will deliver trust in self, each other, and the future.

OUTCOMES

The 6ᵗʰ Degree

OUTCOMES

The 6th Degree

The **Sixth Degree** is the finale of your performance. The success of all of the energy you have invested in building leadership, creating strategic plans, researching new ideas, and marketing people and products is evidenced in the outcomes of profit, position in the market, and your client's achievements.

In the **Sixth Degree,** we suggest a mindset which never allows the process and routine to rob you of your talent. To achieve a position of leadership in any market, we must always question the investment made to achieve a desired level of performance. Continually ask yourself what you do well and what you can improve upon. You will effectively increase utilization of resources and your ability to take on risk in the future if you focus on linking your **Six Degrees** and concentrate on your outcomes.

THE YARD "STICK"

THE YARD "STICK"

One Sunday afternoon, we were driving through the mountains on our way to visit a client who had asked us to evaluate his management style. We were both a little homesick. During the long drive, we reminisced about some of our childhood experiences. We realized that we missed the yards we played in as children. Let's be honest, those were real yards. What happened to the days prior to thatching, weeding, and aerating? We longed for the days of dandelion-infested yards. As kids, we just opened the door and ran out to play on those seasoned tarps of dreams.

Today, almost every yard is an attempt at Augusta National. We don't know whether to mow our lawns in sneakers or golf spikes. Our sheds and garages house multiple bags of chemicals and assorted tools we use to manage and, in some cases, mangle our lawns. We missed those dandelions and the game of "You Like Butter". We were taught to hold a dandelion under our friend's chin. If the sunlight reflected off the flower and onto their chin, the dandelion legend said they were a lover of butter. Now, as lawn owners, we go on a shameless hunt to eliminate these colorful yardsticks of yesterday. We feel for all the children who will never pick a natural dandelion bouquet and lay it at their mother's doorstep.

As we prepared for this particular consult, we decided to pay honor to our youth and leave the dandelions alone. We chose to see the colleagues of today as the dandelions of yesterday. We were determined to use every organizational dandelion. Our duty was to protect the colleagues from managers who could not see beauty and purpose in weeds and flowers. It's easy to spray corporate weed killer and make every organization appear the same. It is more difficult to care for a lawn where weed, flower, and grass all grow together. The result is a corporate yard, versus the company lawn, that is truly a playground for dreams.

However, the bad news is the gardener of this yard had a different plan. He wanted his corporate yard to be a lawn that looked and acted the same. The colleagues struggled to fight the weed killer, but could not survive the chemical agents of pressure and conformity. We tried to show the gardener our plan, which would toughen his lawn and protect it against future revenue drought. At first light, we were weeded from the lawn.

One year later, the entire lawn had died. The most creative dandelions had left and only the robotic blades of the old turf remained. The board of directors was discouraged and weeded the gardener. Their corporate yard had become a barren dirt lot. We were brought back to seed the yard and, after several plantings, the dandelions returned and flourished. Some of the weeds were even placed in charge of the old turf. Together, they have become a field of dreams for clients and colleagues.

When we turn an organization from a lawn of uniformity into a corporate yard, we build a healthy playground where there are no turf wars.

In business, we often apply process and procedure at the expense of creativity. When children run onto a yard, they create games. When we build the corporate yard, we refuse to grow lawns that look the same to everyone. Clients and colleagues will play on our yard because they can finally be children. If we play with creativity at work, work and play become the same healthy yard. Our yardstick begins to measure the height of success rather than the length of failure.

BREAKING THE CODE OF SILENCE

BREAKING THE CODE OF SILENCE

You can find it in any environment where people depend on each other. It can be found in a team member who isn't pulling their weight, an aging parent who denies they need assistance, or a company losing business. Often times, people respond to circumstances with the code of silence. Although it is intended to protect individuals from attack, harm, or panic, the code is ultimately destructive. The code of silence avoids reality only to support delusion and false hope. When an organization first begins to consider evaluating performance outcomes, it is like breaking the code of silence.

Break the code of silence and you will remove excuses to reveal true performance. The whispers of blame will begin to quiet as responsibility is placed where every colleague stands.

It doesn't matter whether performance needs to be addressed in marketing, finance, management, or service delivery because the challenge remains the same. Create an open environment receptive to feedback and planned improvement and positive growth will follow.

We are inevitably faced with breaking the code when we help an organization build an outcomes program. It takes a commitment from all levels and the dedication of resources to make it work. Some leaders may have already established a culture of open communication where everyone has been encouraged to share and solicit feedback from others regarding performance. It isn't until they begin to methodically evaluate practices and service delivery that inconsistencies are uncovered.

The objections to using performance outcomes are standard. "You can't truly measure the impact we create in our business." "Statistics can be manipulated to say whatever you want." "We've never had to justify our existence in the past." If you remove the excuses, you will expose understated achievements and performance potential.

Question your results and think through the answers. Avoid constructing complicated solutions for simple problems. Evaluating outcomes will enable you to shape quality and eliminate production cramps. Organizational muscle will be strengthened because strategies are designed to improve productivity.

Evaluating outcomes will break the code of silence in your industry. As the need to distinguish your business increases, you will begin to measure your performance with the same measuring stick as competitors. Although others may provide the same product or service, it is the delivery that will set you apart. Believe in the talents and skills of your colleagues and their desire to be the best. The greatest challenges lie in helping people to believe in their own abilities. Once we can move past the fear of daily consequences, problems become opportunities and mistakes become lessons.

As leaders, we must create a code of candor when faced with a major loss. Instead of protecting others from bad news, share the results and use them to build new opportunities. You will no longer think about what could have been and only look forward to imagine what you will become. Break the code of silence and you will find success.

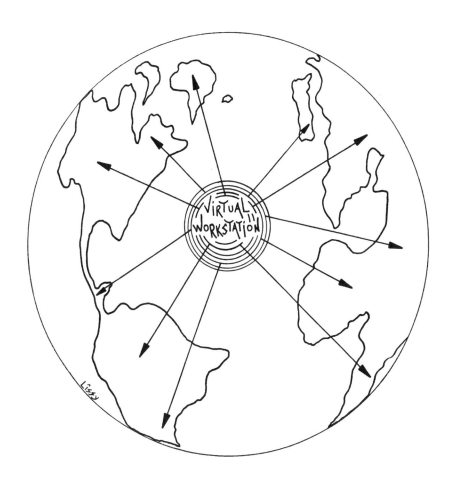

VIRTUAL WORKSTATIONS

VIRTUAL WORKSTATIONS

Preventative maintenance on equipment has become standard practice in most industries. In the past, production lines used to run machines until they dropped because "down time" resulted in increased overhead costs and decreased production. In the airline industry, preventative maintenance is the only way to maintain the safe operation of an aircraft. Shutting down for short periods of time to perform minor scheduled maintenance procedures prevents major breakdowns and fatal crashes.

If we dedicate the same amount of resources to maintaining our colleagues as the airline industry allocates for their planes, we can progress from standing where we work to working wherever we stand.

In a virtual factory, productivity is not limited to standing at your workstation. You have the ability to influence results from the backroom to the boardroom because your virtual workstation is wherever you stand. Transfer any ego invested in office or title into building a virtual workstation for yourself. If you lose your bearings, just check your client compass for their needs and you will know exactly where to stand.

Virtual workstations still require preventative maintenance. Evaluation of the factors that influence individual performance is ongoing, so take the time to perform periodic minor maintenance tasks even when things seem to be running well. Coach performance through frequent and specific feedback. The virtual workstation supports individuals to enter independent or joint ventures and focuses management on developing ownership for others. Reward imagination and initiative. Reinforce priorities and neutralize personnel problems. If you wait for the problem to occur, you have already experienced "down time". Maintain your virtual workstations and the barriers will come down. Eventually, there will be no obstacles to your continued achievement.

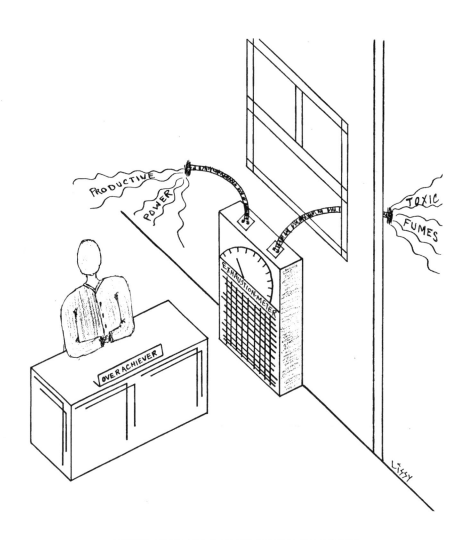

THE EXHAUSTION PIPE

THE EXHAUSTION PIPE

A friend of ours was experiencing constant physical pain and decided to go to the doctor for treatment. Without the use of any medical tests, the doctor diagnosed him with a stress-related virus and suggested he consider de-stressing his life. Despite his recent professional success and wonderful family, he began to doubt his own ability to take it all on. When it was suggested the doctor had misdiagnosed him and he might only have a strain that would improve with rest, he was stumped. He had not even considered the doctor might be wrong.

This happens to us all. The more fatigued we become, the more likely we are to accept what we hear or read without question. Someone restricts the airflow to our exhaustion pipe and we can't think straight. After a week, our friend called and said he felt great. All of the symptoms the doctor had predicted never appeared.

Most overachievers have questioned their ability to take it all on. It doesn't matter whether you are the president of a family-owned business or a Fortune 500 company. Suddenly, you begin to wonder if you really have the right stuff to stay focused under pressure and produce effective results. Someone might have said you look tired or you may have been sick. Although life is going well, others question your ability to keep up the pace and warn you of the inevitable toll your drive will take on your body and your life.

Doubt enters your mind and you wonder if others are right. Could this be the breaking point? The point where the threat of exhaustion convinces you to cut back on your dreams and settle for what you have accomplished? Toxic fumes from the exhaustion of others are trying to contaminate your performance by fueling any insecurity you may have. When the airflow in your exhaustion pipe is not sufficient, your productive power is reduced to running on fumes. Restricted airflow has unexpectedly knocked some leaders off their feet. If you feel like you have more problems than solutions, look for the leaks in your exhaust system.

Install high performance exhaustion pipes to eliminate the toxic fumes of doubt that may restrict you from breathing new creative energy.

Failure is not an option because you can't conceive living any other way except full bore. The drains of the past and present can create drag and reduce your future speed. Look for the drains on your energy. Focus on surrounding yourself with people and challenges that fuel your internal fire. Increase creative airflow to the human intake, install your exhaustion pipe, and remove all excuses.

With the installation of an efficient exhaustion pipe, you will be able to eliminate toxic fumes and open your intake to finding opportunity in every day and advantage in every problem. Always question the norm and seek to move opportunity forward.

DELAY OF GAME

DELAY OF GAME

Imagine you are competing in the playoffs to earn a shot at the championship. You are at the finals and may lose the final match due to delay of game. Regardless of the cause, delay of game attempts to stall the rhythm of progress and achievement.

Your opponents and fellow teammates may contribute to the game delays that are often encountered in competition. These delays are spurred on by the fear of success more than the fear of failure. Although both have the power to defeat potential, the fear of success is often the product of uncertainty.

When potential is procrastinated, performance is sacrificed. It is hesitation of the heart that undermines the ultimate performance.

Players may fake injuries or cause a foul to stall the clock while coaches may delay strategic decisions until they can regroup with the team in the locker room. When a business leader is not prepared to make a decision, they will cause a delay of game.

Success doesn't come from just playing the game. It comes from resources necessary to play the game, pursue goals, and break records. When faced with indecision, apply the pressure of the penalty box. Call on the player or coach to either make a move or forfeit the game.

Sometimes players will delay the game to change the pace of play to their advantage. When attention is drawn to our flaws, our focus shifts away from achieving the goal to doubting success. Distractions can threaten our game if they cause us to hesitate. Deny hesitation and you will respond to the pressure of accountability with the motivation to succeed. The confidence to move forward eliminates the fear of criticism found when trying new plays.

Use concentration to convert the inactivity of game delays into an opportunity to question reality and look for the competitive edge.

Question your reality rather than yourself and believe in the obviousness of the truth. Players are most vulnerable to losing focus when the game is slow. Never doubt yourself. The skills you had before the game delay will still be there when play resumes. Continue to focus on the skill and the results will eventually follow.

SMOKING THE QUITTING HABIT

SMOKING THE QUITTING HABIT

We have all known people who have tried to quit the habit of smoking. Often times, it is not a pretty sight. On the surface, it seems so simple for someone to just give up a bad habit. Just stop the habit and quit cold turkey! Unfortunately, this strategy doesn't work for many. Just as an addiction may be tough to break, the quitting habit is not much different. You can find it in any environment. When faced with the challenge of reaching for peak performance, the quitting habit keeps someone from delivering on their potential.

Break the quitting habit one step at a time by finding the fear of success, putting it in the pipe of excuses, and watch the habit of quitting go up in smoke.

People often resort to quitting because they fear stepping outside of their comfort zone and seek to avoid the pressure to perform at the next level. To help someone break the addiction of quitting, give them small achievable tasks to build up their confidence. Show them others with similar skill packages that have been able to achieve a higher level. Share with them that success is a challenge even for overachievers. Provide them with opportunities to engage in collegial partnerships minimizing inexperience.

Before you begin the challenge, map out your strategies with everyone's input to establish ownership in the achievement. Try to make the endeavor fun and seek to instill some form of entertainment. You can always find the opportunity for comic relief no matter how tough the situation. When faced with a large challenge, break it into smaller successes to achieve the main goal. Use a personal journal to document the achievements of others and to develop reminders for future goals.

If you fall short of the goal, admit the failure and build from it instead of rationalizing with excuses. You should know when to confront the quitter. There are times when confrontation is necessary and others when it can appear to be as overwhelming to the quitter as the challenge itself. Break down the strategies and coach the quitter one step at a time. Know their benchmarks and decide when it is best to change direction. Every achievement is the kindling that starts the fire burning away self-doubt. The following are fire starters that smoke the quitting habit:

♦ Call on mentors to support the pursuit of the goal
♦ Present the challenge in clear terms to focus on strategies for success
♦ Grant room for mistakes
♦ Support solid decision-making with consistent execution
♦ Always choose persistence
♦ Failure is not an option!

When peak performance is finally delivered, recognize it with the magnitude of its impact on the goal. Give equal recognition to those who delivered their best game and lost as you would to those who won. Plan to succeed and only quit when you finish everything you start.

THE NEGATIVE ZONE

THE NEGATIVE ZONE

We have always loved *The Twilight Zone.* As kids, we thought *The Twilight Zone* existed only on television. After decades of working in business, we have realized *The Twilight Zone* really does exist because we have been forced to travel into it. It is the place we refer to as The Negative Zone. Although The Negative Zone doesn't have Rod Serling, it can be just as entertaining.

Some leaders have difficulty becoming involved with profit. They fear it will become the motive rather than the means, eventually drawing them into The Negative Zone. They resort to using their anti-profit weapons of process and routine. The process becomes more important than the product and no contingency plans are developed. Speaking of profit is considered taboo and the 'Hoping for the Best' management model becomes the plan for survival.

Whether for-profit or non-profit, every organization strives for profitable results impacting their client. All of the successful profit prophets we know have the ability to face their weaknesses and welcome critical thinking from colleagues. Never accept weaknesses or threats because your competitors are faced with the same circumstances. The objective is to build a sandbox in which everyone wants to play.

We have met several process prophets drawn to considering the problem rather than developing the solution. If given more power and control, they have the means for doing more damage than good without even knowing it. Finances are managed to control expenses rather than generate new revenue. The organization becomes their personal anti-profit weapon. It is the void they emerge from and the place they return to when the deal dies. If they are drawn closer and closer to the zone, they will travel further into the void than they realize. The Negative Zone draws them in and, eventually, causes them to close their doors.

When you find yourself in The Negative Zone, everyday assumptions are inverted. It is most recognizable as a place where things don't quite turn out like they should. Most organizations have drifted into this zone at some point in their existence.

A nationally known and revered leader gave us the opportunity to see what it was like inside The Negative Zone. When this man was outside of the zone, he appeared to be a leader and visionary. When he was forced to be accountable for profit, he entered The Negative Zone and became inefficient, indecisive, and insecure. He soon realized concentrating on profit would produce creativity and vision.

To avoid The Negative Zone, we must erase the line between for-profits and non-profits. The only real difference between the two is how profit is distributed. Never avoid profit to take a loss. If you do, you cheat yourself of opportunity and allow process and routine to drive decision-making. Evaluate your initiatives by the impact they will have on your survival and growth. If they are critical to survival, place high priority on the resources allocated for their success. If a project incurs more deficits than benefits, it should receive low priority. Your agenda will no longer be driven by due dates. It will be focused on achieving a mission with a margin.

Drive your priorities to respond to opportunity rather than deadlines. Manage your time by your priorities and your resources will return maximum impact on your investment.

If we keep profit in context, we can all stay out of The Negative Zone. The profit prophet realizes you will never arrive if you stop to worship the road leading to your destination. If you delay your travels to complain, you will never make any real progress. When the road of profit follows your beliefs and your final destination is your mission, your travels will lead you to The Positive Zone.

FRESH PRODUCE

FRESH PRODUCE

Fresh production is the one outcome that can be counted on to motivate an organization. New production overcomes most problems and revitalizes everyone. However, a strong strategic plan does not necessarily ensure production. It is the result of determination and hustle. Great producers ensure production by finding ways to energize their organization.

Eventually, every organization must face the time when profit is not at an acceptable level. As leaders, we can do everything possible to control expenses. However, there has never been an organization that has saved its way to prosperity.

Fresh production is the key to unlocking exciting opportunity and consistent profit.

When times are tough, it is often difficult to sustain production. Producers can feel such intense pressure that they eventually become frozen by indecision. This indecision perpetuates the confusion accompanying rough times. When an organization faces adversity, the excuses end up flowing quicker than the profits. Instead of working to increase production, everyone is quick to find the reason for poor performance.

Many members of management talk the great game of production. Yet instead of setting sail for the land of production, they often stay safe at harbor. They find it easier to point the way than to take the helm and produce. Leaders find the strength necessary to lead in both good times and bad. They understand their main priority is to produce successful outcomes for the organization.

We find it humorous to hear the cry to return to basics in the middle of the delivery on a strategic plan. What are the basics? The basics are changed and reformatted forever at the exact moment a strategic plan sets out to achieve new outcomes. The surest way to bankrupt the future is to go back to basics. There is no back. When trying to develop fresh production and profit, the only way to go is forward.

When the organization is stale, there are several steps necessary to deliver fresh production. Give clearly focused objectives to your marketing colleagues. Personally challenge the top producers to achieve solid and timely success. Since they are your elite team, they will respond to tough challenges. Place new producers into a one-on-one mentoring assignment with seasoned veterans. New producers may be facing adversity for the first time and will find it necessary to be encouraged and led by a veteran. When your top producers begin to feel responsibility for the success of their protégé, they will also excel.

There are no titles in the match of winning back the number one market position. Lead as though there is no tomorrow. Attack the day as if the arrival of night signals the end of the game. Great producers do not believe you win some and lose some. They believe you win some and you totally dominate the others. If you take time to breathe in the air around you, you can smell the freshness of production no matter how the wind of challenge is blowing.

FORWARD

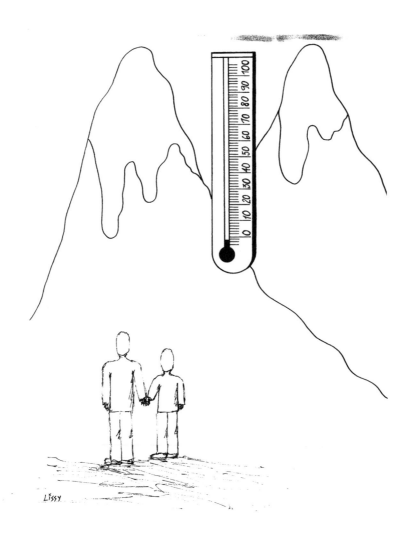

BELOW ZERO

BELOW ZERO

Most of us have had the experience of feeling intense cold. The memory of frozen fingertips and toes so cold we were sure they were frost bitten instantly comes to mind upon hearing the words "below zero". When faced with deep freeze, there comes a point when we become resigned to the pain and surrender to the cold. Survivors of icy disasters recall calmness when the end was near.

It was a bitter cold day in December. My father and I were deer hunting in the beautiful mountains of Pennsylvania. We had arrived in the forest well before the sun had time to appear. Dad had always trained me to wear layers of clothing to create the most warmth. After forty-five minutes, I was convinced there were not enough layers on the planet for this day.

The wind was biting my skin. The arrival of a snowstorm was a welcomed event because it provided visual proof everything had not yet frozen solid. I constantly surveyed my watch face hoping noon would come at 7:45 am because I knew Dad and I would meet then. I was sure he had to be as cold as I was and the hunt would end early.

As I heard the sound of Dad's feet crunching over the frozen earth behind my deer stand, I actually felt my body getting warmer. When I saw him, his face was excited and alive with energy. He explained how he had just spotted a herd of deer and was convinced he could drive them toward my position if I could wait for another hour or two. With a concerned look, he asked "Are you cold?" The excitement and energy Dad had created made me feel warm and ready to go. I replied, "Are you kidding Dad? Let's do some hunting." As he walked away, I was shocked to notice I had removed my right glove. Throughout the story, father and son had been holding hands.

On that brutally cold December day, my father and I had a successful hunt. We laughed and practically strolled off the mountaintop. I haven't been hunting since Dad died. I guess the cold bothers me more now than it used to.

In our home and business, the temperature can drop below zero. The lack of opportunity and excitement can create a frozen wasteland. We must all hunt as Dad did for the event, fueling a natural fire in our hearts.

Leaders should track and drive the game to those who have become frozen from the cold of inactivity.

Certainly, there are times when the workplace can appear just like the frozen tundra. The routine at home can serve as a cold reminder of the danger of monotony. Success and achievement finds people holding hands in below zero conditions. We rally to the thrill of the hunt and warm from the internal energy it creates.

I believe I'll start to hunt again. I have learned we can't expect others to survive below zero conditions if we refuse to listen for the footsteps of challenge crunching on the snow.

— Anthony C. Gruppo

About the Authors...

Anthony C. Gruppo

Anthony C. Gruppo, the founder of Lehr Management Corporation and The Lehr Institute, leads a national marketing, consulting and organizational development firm. He is considered a futurist, and is highly sought-after as a keynote speaker in national and international arenas. Anthony's visionary and innovative strategies have enabled clients to look beyond their own survival to building success for their customers. Anthony designed and published *The Infranet Model*, a managed care workbook and seminar series, which has provided children's residential programs with the framework to prepare for entry into new markets. Anthony's first book, *Creating Reality - A Guide to Personal Accomplishment*, has become the handbook for many organizations on teaching employees to think like owners. He also co-authored *Under Construction* with Nick Bollettieri, world famous tennis coach, which combines the world of sports and business to develop your ultimate personal and professional game.

Monique ter Haar

Monique ter Haar, of Lehr Management Corporation and The Lehr Institute, has a diverse background in organizational development, business, psychology, and anthropology. Described by many as a corporate clinician, she has provided consulting services that range from building creative mentoring programs for national networks to designing management models for multi-national corporations. Her broad range of experience provides practical perspectives that look past just managing change to building custom-made platforms for future growth. Monique focuses her efforts on designing interventions for non-profit and for-profit organizations, which facilitate parallel growth and total integration, resulting in speed of operations and competitive edge.

The Lehr Institute presents
an innovative & interactive new seminar...

Six Degrees of Impact: Breaking Corporate Glass

In a time when many organizations are becoming more dependent on consulting services, Anthony and Monique believe we should build our strengths and create opportunity from the inside-out. The *Six Degrees of Impact* seminar positions you and your organization to gain new ground in business by breaking traditional corporate glass and creating high-impact zones. The *Six Degrees* seminar shows you how to create long-term vision through an innovative framework that positions you to achieve futuristic goals. The result is increased focus and change designed to manage risk and maximize your individual and organizational performance.

To learn more, contact Monique or Anthony at one of the following:

> **Phone:** 800-634-8237
> **E-mail:** anthony.gruppo@hslehr.com
> monique.terhaar@hslehr.com

First Degree
"Leadership"

NOTES

Second Degree
"Strategic Positioning"

NOTES

Third Degree
"Research & Development"

NOTES

Fourth Degree
"Marketing"

NOTES